RSPB
TREES OF THE
BRITISH ISLES

A photographic identification guide

GABRIEL HEMERY

B L O O M S B U R Y   W I L D L I F E

LONDON · OXFORD · NEW YORK · NEW DELHI · SYDNEY

BLOOMSBURY WILDLIFE
Bloomsbury Publishing Plc
50 Bedford Square, London, WC1B 3DP, UK
Bloomsbury Publishing Ireland Limited,
29 Earlsfort Terrace, Dublin 2, D02 AY28, Ireland

BLOOMSBURY, BLOOMSBURY WILDLIFE and
the Diana logo are trademarks of Bloomsbury
Publishing Plc

First published in the United Kingdom 2026

Bloomsbury Publishing Plc does not have any
control over, or responsibility for, any third-party
websites referred to or in this book. All internet
addresses given in this book were correct at the
time of going to press. The author and publisher
regret any inconvenience caused if addresses
have changed or sites have ceased to exist,
but can accept no responsibility
for any such changes.

No responsibility for loss caused to any
individual or organisation acting on or refraining
from action as a result of the material in this
publication can be accepted by Bloomsbury
or the author.

A catalogue record for this book is available
from the British Library. Library of Congress
Cataloguing-in-Publication data has been
applied for.

ISBN: PB: 978-1-3994-2241-3;
ePub: 978-1-3994-2244-4;
ePDF: 978-1-3994-2243-7

10 9 8 7 6 5 4 3 2 1

Designed by Austin Taylor
Typeset in Acumin Variable Condensed
Printed and bound in Turkey by Elma Basim

100%
From well-
managed forests
FSC® C164814

To find out more about our authors and books
visit www.bloomsbury.com and sign up for our
newsletters. For product safety related questions
contact productsafety@bloomsbury.com.

For all licensed products sold
by Bloomsbury Publishing PLC,
Bloomsbury Publishing PLC will
donate a minimum of 2% from all
sales to RSPB Sales Ltd, which gives all its
distributable profits through Gift Aid to the
RSPB. Subsequent sellers of this book are
not commercial participators for the purpose
of Part II of the Charities Act 1992.

Contents

Introduction

The natural landscapes and emerald character of the British Isles are shaped and enhanced by trees. While we have fewer native trees than many countries, our moist and oceanic conditions mean we play host to rare temperate rainforests. Equally, our varied conditions mean that we've been able to introduce trees from right across the world, from the Pacific coast of North America to continental Europe, to China and Australia.

This guide includes more than 90 tree species that you are most likely to spot in Britain and Ireland, whether growing in a fragment of precious ancient woodland or rare temperate rainforest, emerging from a lonely crag, shading your favourite walk or gracing a city park.

If there were no trees in the world, it would not only look very different, but the planet would support very much less life. It is no exaggeration to say that humans emerged from the trees many millennia ago, and that ever since, trees have nurtured us from cradle to grave. Yet, over time, as our way of living has become ever more sophisticated, we have lost our deeper connections with nature.

Today, most of us would not know the best leaves to cut for livestock fodder, or the best wood to warm us in a winter fire or use for the spokes of a cartwheel, but that doesn't mean trees and their timber are no longer important to us — far from it. Vast quantities of wood products are used today in constructing buildings, while timber remains a material of choice for quality furniture. Trees produce many of our favourite nuts and fruits. They also help protect soils, green our towns and cities, reduce flooding, and provide invaluable homes to wildlife. When grown sustainably, locking up carbon as they

↑ Stem of young Monkey Puzzle.

mature, trees have a vital role to play in the climate emergency.

Observing trees, whether in a semi-natural woodland, park, arboretum or garden, can help us all reconnect with nature. Looking closely at a tree's bark, leaves or flowers inevitably inspires a sense of awe and wonder. Being able to identify a tree is more than just giving it a name — your new-found knowledge will unlock an appreciation of nature and a deeper and more meaningful connection with the natural world. Not only will you understand more about habitats and ecosystems, but it can also help ground you, fostering a deeper sense of purpose and meaning in life. Go forth and explore!

← European Beech in summer.

Pedunculate Oak.

How to use this guide

Geography

This guide focuses on tree species found growing in Britain and Ireland, collectively known as the British Isles. There are many terms in use to describe the geography of the two islands of Britain and Ireland, which can cause confusion. For the avoidance of doubt, in this text 'Britain' is used as shorthand for Great Britain, which includes the nations of England, Scotland and Wales. Ireland is used to mean the island of Ireland, comprising Northern Ireland and the Republic of Ireland, the latter referred to as Éire in this text.

Species descriptions

More than 90 individual tree species are described in detail, and many more are mentioned, adopting the most appropriate common name (other names are often described in the text entries), followed by a scientific name. Symbols highlight key features.

↓ Foliage of Giant Redwood.

Native status in Britain/Ireland
(see p.18):

native to
Britain

native to
Ireland

non-native

Conifer or broadleaved:

conifer

broadleaved

Evergreen or deciduous:

evergreen

deciduous

Special value:

biodiversity:
the value
of a tree to
other forms of
wildlife

landscape:
the visual
and amenity
benefits of
tree

timber:
timber and
other related
woody
products
derived from
a tree

Tree size:

Small:
up to 15m

Medium:
15–30m

Large:
30m+

TEXT ENTRIES

Biology A short description including a species taxonomy, plus distribution and reproduction.

Identification Key features including tree size and shape, bark, shoots and buds, leaves, flowers and fruit/cones. Comparisons are provided with other species that may be easily confused.

Culture A description of a tree's preferred habitat and/or growing environment,

↑ Female cones of European Larch.

plus notes on propagation, nurturing and aftercare, and highlights of cultural uses.

Biodiversity General value to wildlife and highlights of associated biodiversity.

Threats General notes about threats to the species, whether from human activities, or pests and pathogens.

PHOTOGRAPHS

The main feature photograph for each species entry generally illustrates a whole tree or other key distinguishing feature. Tree shape and stature can vary hugely, as the environment a tree grows in heavily influences these aspects. For example, a specimen growing on an open field generally has a broad spreading crown, but the same species in a forest is likely to be tall and narrow as it reaches for light in the canopy. Exposure from wind and altitude also affects tree shape and stature. Other images illustrate key features to aid with identification, such as bark, leaves, flowers and fruits. Again, these can vary considerably, especially leaf size, which is dependent on light levels and exposure. Photographs of typical specimens have been provided.

Tree watching

Tree watching is a wonderful pastime. It may not have the more obvious allure of some wildlife watching hobbies, but as you learn, you will soon find yourself drawn into the silvan world. Appreciating trees may also give you a deeper appreciation of the myriad living things that depend on trees for their survival, including birds, mammals, invertebrates, fungi, lichens, mosses, liverworts and more!

With a little practice you can learn a huge amount about a tree or woodland by observing closely – not just the identity of a tree but an understanding of why it is growing and 'behaving' like it is. In fact, it's a little bit like learning to read; you can learn the skills to 'read a tree' and learn to 'read a woodland'.

Location is always important in helping you to identify a tree, from where you

↑ Guelder Rose fruits.

are in the country down to the very local conditions. Some tree species are quite uncommon or even absent from certain locations in Britain and Ireland. Notice whether the tree is growing at high altitude, exposed to sea winds on the coast, or in polluted urban areas, as some species are more hardy or tolerant than others. Foresters study soils as they are so important in growing healthy trees. While you may not be interested in soil texture, or know how to tell whether a soil is acid or alkaline, you can quite easily tell if the tree is growing in a wet place, or notice if there are lots of other vigorous plants growing nearby, which indicates a fertile soil.

Seasonal variation adds another dimension to tree watching. It's not always the case that winter identification is more challenging, because the absence of leaves in a tree can reveal more about its form. Evergreen and deciduous forms become more obvious during winter months. Early flowering before any leaves appear in spring, or fruits persisting after leaves have fallen in autumn, are often helpful signs, too.

← Turkey Oak leaves.

Management has a significant impact on how a tree or woodland might appear. If you spot a tree with multiple stems growing from the ground, this could be a coppice stool or part of an ancient traditionally laid hedge. A very straight tree stem without side branches might be the result of decades of careful pruning by a forester to create high-value timber; look carefully and you may even see the scars left behind as subtle swirls in its bark. If you can spot straight lines of space between trees in a woodland, or if all the trees appear to be a similar age, these are signs that it is a fairly modern plantation. In contrast, if there is a good variety of tree species, of different ages and statures, and no obvious straight lines between them, then the woodland is more likely to be semi-natural, or even ancient in origin.

You can bring all your senses to bear when tree watching: sight, smell, sound, touch and taste are all useful when identifying species.

Sight is most obvious. You can learn to appreciate the importance of local conditions when you read a tree. Is it growing under shade? If so, this might be a good clue that it is shade-tolerant. You may also notice how leaf size is much larger in shade than in sunlight. How has the tree responded to the local environment? Has it been

→ London Plane trees.

bent by prevailing winds, has it had to grow outwards to reach sufficient light? Has it been impacted by browsing deer or squirrels? What other trees or plants are growing nearby? How would you describe the colour and surface of a tree's leaves: simply 'green', or more precisely glossy blue-green or downy pale green? You may want to use an app on your phone or carry a handheld magnifying glass to spot microscopic features, like tiny hairs underneath a leaf, or the parts of a flower.

Smell is more important than you may imagine. Sometimes, smell can be one of the first things you notice when standing under a particular tree or when entering

a forest. Rubbing leaves or bark can be really helpful when identifying a tree. Trees can be highly fragrant (for example, the flowers of Black Locust or the foliage of Western Red Cedar), while less pleasant – even pungent – smells can be distinctive (for example, flowers of the Wayfaring-tree or the foliage of Box)!

Sound is perhaps the least obvious sense you can bring to bear when tree watching, but should not be overlooked. On a spring walk, you may hear the hum of bees and hoverflies feeding on the flowers of Goat Willow before you reach the tree. Stand beneath the canopy of an Aspen in a light summer breeze and enjoy the unmistakable trembling of its leaves. On a hot day, listen to the cracking of seed pods splitting open on Common Gorse or Black Locust.

Touch and feel are also important. Press a tree stem to check the sponginess of bark – this helps differentiate between Giant Redwood and Japanese Red Cedar. Run your fingers gently over the surface or margin of a leaf to judge whether it has hairs. Spiky, downy, sharp, blunt and more can all help when differentiating between similar species.

Finally, taste can be very satisfying when enjoying familiar tree fruits. But remember: just because a berry or seed looks enticing, this doesn't mean it is necessarily good for you to eat. In fact, many tree species have toxic bark, foliage, fruits or berries, and can be very dangerous if ingested. Take notice of any cautionary notes in the species descriptions.

↓ European Beech trees line an ancient holloway.

↑ Black Alder.

Botanical names

Tree names can be baffling. Often several different common names can apply to a single tree species, and even a variety of regional names, which can be endearing but also confusing. Then there are true firs, false cypresses and other unclear terms. This is because common names evolve over time, whether by accidental misnaming, misidentification, or deliberate and creative renaming for marketing reasons. Compared to other taxa, with trees there is further room for confusion arising from the naming of timber, which can be chaotic!

Just a few examples of the many confusing common names for trees:

• Western Red Cedar belongs to the cypress family, and is not closely related to true cedars such as Cedar of Lebanon, Deodar and Atlas Cedar.

• Initially botanists classified Douglas-fir as a hemlock (genus *Tsuga*), and later thought it a fir (like European Silver Fir, Grand Fir or Noble Fir), but it is now recognised as a member of the pine family, hence the hyphen in its common name and its genus *Pseudotsuga*, which means 'like a hemlock'.

• Rowan is sometimes known as Mountain Ash (but is not closely related to Common Ash).

• Giant Redwood is also known as Wellingtonia in Britain, as it was introduced soon after the death of the Duke of Wellington (1769–1852). The same tree is also known to Americans as the Washingtonia tree to commemorate President George Washington (1732–1799).

- Black Locust is sometimes called Robinia (its genus name) or False Acacia (an English translation of its species name).
- Common names differ between languages, often due to patriotic reasons. For example, some people may refer to Pedunculate Oak as English Oak, yet in Germany the same species may be called Deutsche Eiche (German Oak).
- 'Deal' is an obsolete unit of measurement for timber, hence the town of Deal in Kent, where ships used to offload timber imported from the continent. In the timber trade, the term 'white deal' is sometimes still used for spruce or true fir timbers, while 'red deal' refers to pine. Meanwhile, Port Orford Cedar is the timber name for Lawson's Cypress (i.e. it's not a cedar).

↑ Sweet Chestnut leaves.

Why scientific names rule

Given the confusion of common names, a scientific name is the only 'safe' way to clearly describe any particular tree species. Scientific names can initially appear complicated. Yet, with a little perseverance and learning, gaining some familiarity of scientific names can not only reduce confusion, but also reveal how one species is related to another.

It's true that scientific names can change over time as our understanding of taxonomy has advanced, particularly with the arrival of DNA studies. The main difference compared to common names is that any changes in scientific naming are documented in published literature. This means that changes in a scientific name can be followed through time. In theory, there should only ever be one accepted current scientific name in use (although in some cases botanists may still disagree!).

The main elements of a scientific name

There are many levels or divisions used to describe the classification of plants, and this hierarchical system is known as plant taxonomy. In this guide, the main high-level groups of angiosperms and gymnosperms are used, and occasionally the term 'families' is mentioned to describe closely related genera (see below).

The main scientific names given in this text are the genus (plural: genera) and species. The scientific name most familiar to readers is likely to be the name used to describe human beings: *Homo sapiens*. Note how both words are written in italics, first the genus (*Homo*) using a leading capital, followed by the species (*sapiens*) all in lower case. Back to trees, in the example *Fraxinus excelsior* for Common Ash, then *Fraxinus* is the genus and *excelsior* the species. We can now understand that so-called 'Mountain Ash' (Rowan), or *Sorbus aucuparia*, is not closely related to Common Ash because it belongs to a different genus.

To complete details of a scientific name, an 'authority' is normally added at the end, which refers to the scientist(s) who first published the name, typically in abbreviated form. The founder of this system was Swedish botanist Carl Linnaeus (1707–1778). For example, many tree species carry 'L.' after their scientific name (for example, *Fraxinus excelsior* L.) to recognise Linnaeus as the authority. In this guide, authorities have been deliberately omitted to simplify the text.

Other elements of a scientific name

Sometimes other elements can be included alongside a genus and species. These describe further subdivisions, for example to describe variations that are not distinct enough to deserve classification at species level.

- **subsp.** – subspecies, for example *Pinus nigra* subsp. *laricio* (Corsican Pine), where *laricio* is a subspecies of Black Pine (*Pinus nigra*).
- **var.** – a naturally occurring variety, for example *Populus nigra* var. *italica* (Lombardy Poplar), where *italica* is a variety of Black Poplar (*Pinus nigra*).
- **agg.** – abbreviation for aggregate, signifying a group of closely related species that are treated as a single, combined species for practical purposes, for example *Ulmus minor* agg. for field elm.
- **cultivar** – a cultivated variety of a species, normally in plain text with inverted commas after the species, for example *Juglans regia* 'Lara' (a nut-

producing variety of Common Walnut).
- **✗** – used to describe a hybrid between two species, for example, *Platanus* × *hispanica* is a naturally occurring hybrid between *Platanus orientalis* (Oriental Plane) and *Platanus occidentalis* (Western Plane).

Common names

A final word on common names. There is no denying that common names are more accessible for most people. Often there are many options to choose from, and in this guide the intention has been to choose a common name that is most descriptive and least confusing. A good example is adopting 'Pedunculate Oak' rather than the 'patriotic' form of 'English Oak', as it borrows a botanical term (peduncle), which helps describe the species' form.

↓ Italian Alder catkins.

Botanical terms

The following botanical terms are used sparingly in the species descriptions and keys. While these can appear a little technical, they are worth learning, as they describe very precisely the distinctive features of a tree that can be important in helping to identify it and understanding its nature. Adopting these terms also helps to describe quite detailed attributes in just a word or two. Note, more general terms are described in the Glossary (p.234).

Term	Description
agg.	abbreviation for aggregate, signifying a group of closely related species that are treated as a single, combined species for practical purposes.
alternate	a pattern where buds and leaves grow on alternate sides of a shoot, first one side and then the other (see also **opposite**).
angiosperms	a group of flowering plants that bear their seeds in **fruit**. Plural form is formally written Angiospermae (see also **broadleaved**, **gymnosperms**).
appressed	pressed close to a stem (e.g. as in buds).
aril	a fruit-like structure surrounding a seed of a **gymnosperm**, which is not technically a fruit (e.g. Yew) (see also **fruit**).
axil	the connection between two parts of a tree, as in shoot to **leaf** ('leaf axil'), or leaf midrib to vein ('vein axil').
broadleaved	a general term meaning a tree that has broad and flat leaves, and its seeds are produced inside a fruit, technically an **angiosperm** (see also **conifer**, **gymnosperms**).
catkin	(also ament) a cluster of flowers that are usually without petals and single sex, often hanging but can be upright.
clone (clonal)	a genetically identical replica of a parent tree, from naturally occurring vegetative reproduction (e.g. root suckers) or artificially by taking cuttings.
common name	the name(s) in English (or other languages) commonly given to a tree. Multiple names are commonplace, regionally and nationally, and are not officially registered (see also **scientific name**).
compound (leaf shape)	a type of leaf whose blade is divided into leaflets. Different types of compound leaves include palmate and pinnate (see also **single leaf**).
cone	a seed-bearing organ on **gymnosperm** plants (conifers), technically known as a strobilus.
conifer	a group of **gymnosperm** trees which produce cones (see also **broadleaved**).
corymb	a type of **inflorescence** where multiple individual flowers appear as a flat disc, with outside flowers growing on longer stalks (see also **cyme**).
crenate (leaf margin)	a leaf margin with small rounded or blunt teeth.

Term	Description
cultivar	a type of tree which has been deliberately cultivated for specific traits that are retained when propagated. Usually written after the genus and species within inverted commas, e.g. *Malus domestica* 'Bramley's Seedling' (see also **variety**).
cyme	a flat or rounded inflorescence where the central flower opens first, followed by the surrounding flowers (see also **corymb**).
deciduous	a tree whose foliage dies at the end of the summer, and usually falls off in winter (but not always) (see also **evergreen**).
dentate (leaf margin)	a toothed leaf margin, either single or double-toothed, facing outwards (see also **serrate**).
dicotyledon	a flowering plant that grows with two **seed leaves**. Also shortened to dicot. All 'true trees' are dicotyledons (see also **monocotyledon**).
dioecious	where male and female flowers are borne on separate trees (see also **monoecious**).
double-toothed (leaf margin)	a leaf margin having large teeth with smaller teeth in between.
drupe	a type of **fruit**, sometimes known as a stone fruit, with a central nut or stone surrounded by a fleshy growth, e.g. Common Walnut. A 'druplet' is a small drupe, many of which make up a fruit like a blackberry or raspberry.
elaiosome	a fleshy appendage attached to a seed that is rich in lipids and proteins, serving as a food reward for ants.
entire (leaf margin)	a smooth leaf margin without indentations.
evergreen	a tree whose foliage remains live and green throughout the year (see also **deciduous**).
family	a taxonomic rank comprising groups of similar **genera**.
fascicle	a structure holding together a bundle of pine needles.
flower	a reproductive structure on **angiosperm** trees. Can contain both male and female sexes (hermaphrodite) in the same structure, or male and female flowers can grow as separate structures (see also **cone**).
fruit	a seed-bearing structure in an **angiosperm**, made from a swollen ovary following fertilisation.
genus	a taxonomic rank between **family** and **species**, containing closely related species. Plural is genera.
gymnosperms	a group of plants that produce seeds which are naked, being unprotected within an ovary or **fruit**. Plural form is formally written Gymnospermae (see also **conifer**, **angiosperms**).
hybrid (hybridise)	an offspring resulting from crossbreeding of two different **tree species** or **subspecies**. Scientific naming inserts an '×', e.g. *Platanus* × *hispanica* (London Plane).
inflorescence	a cluster of individual **flowers**.

Term	Description
keel	a structure of some pea-like flowers formed by two fused petals (like the keel of a boat), typically flanked on either side by 'wing' petals.
leaf (pl. leaves)	an important part of a tree for photosynthesis. Leaves can take many forms, whether broad and flat for most **broadleaves**, or thin or scale-like in **conifers**. Collectively, leaves make up the foliage of a tree.
leaf scar	the mark left on a shoot after a leaf falls off, where the leaf **petiole** was attached.
leaflet	a sub-leaf making up part of a **compound leaf**.
lenticel	raised pores on bark (often darker and rougher than surrounding areas), which allow gas exchange between the atmosphere and the internal tissues.
lignotuber	a swelling of the root crown, often visible as woody nodules on the lower trunk, probably a protection against stem damage (e.g. by wildfire).
lobed (leaf margin)	a leaf margin with curved indentations.
lobulated (leaf margin)	a leaf edge that has rounded or pointed lobes.
margin (leaf)	the outside edge of a **leaf** or **leaflet**.
midrib	the central vein of a **leaf**.
monocotyledon	a flowering plant that grows with one seed leaf. Also shortened to monocot. Although some monocotyledon species have 'tree' as part of their common name, they are not 'true trees' (see also **dicotyledon**).
monoecious	where male and female flowers are borne on the same tree. Most conifers are monoecious (see also **dioecious**).
needle (leaf)	a type of leaf found on **conifer** trees, either growing as needles or scale-like foliage.
opposite	a pattern where buds and leaves grow together in pairs on opposite sides of a shoot (see also **alternate**).
palmate	usually used to describe a type of **compound leaf** whose **leaflets** radiate outwards at the end of the **petiole** (like fingers of a hand), e.g. Horse Chestnut. Can also describe a single leaf whose veins radiate outwards, e.g. Sycamore.
panicle	a type of branched inflorescence where the flower clusters themselves are also branched (see also **raceme**).
peduncle	a stalk carrying the **fruit** of an **angiosperm**, e.g. acorns of Pedunculate Oak.
petal	part of a flower surrounding its reproductive organs, often coloured brightly to attract pollinators.
petiole	the stalk of a **leaf**.
pinnate (leaf shape)	a type of **compound leaf** made of multiple **leaflets** arranged either side of a central axis (rachis), e.g. Common Ash.

Term	Description
pome	a type of **fruit** produced by **angiosperm** trees and containing multiple seeds surrounded by fleshy cells (usually edible), e.g. apple fruit.
pulvini	small wooden pegs that bear needles of spruce trees.
raceme	a type of branched inflorescence where multiple individual flowers are attached by short, equal stalks at equal distances along a central stem (see also **panicle**).
samara	a winged seed, e.g. Field Maple.
scale (cone)	part of a **cone** on a **gymnosperm**, usually woody plates but sometimes modified to other forms, e.g. **aril**.
scale (leaf)	overlapping scale-like foliage of some conifers which are flat and often soft, sometimes feathery.
scientific name	an official name of a species, usually in Latin or Greek. Can change over time (e.g. after advances in genetic study) but is officially recognised in literature (see also **common name**).
seed leaf	an embryonic leaf that first emerges from a germinating seed (see also **mono/dicotyledon**).
serrate (leaf margin)	a toothed leaf margin, either single or double-toothed, pointing forwards towards the leaf tip (see also **dentate**).
serrulate (leaf margin)	a leaf margin that is finely toothed.
sessile	sitting on the surface (e.g. a leaf without a **petiole** or a **fruit** without a **peduncle**).
simple (leaf shape)	a single undivided leaf, although it can be variously shaped, e.g. **lobed** or **palmate** (see also **compound**).
species (sp.)	the basic taxonomic rank, below **genus**, and within which two individuals can breed and produce fertile offspring.
subspecies (subsp.)	a taxonomic rank below species, meaning closely related individuals which vary only slightly (e.g. size or shape) but are otherwise very similar, can interbreed. Abbreviated to subsp.
tree	a large plant with a woody stem (technically always a **dicotyledon**).
variegated	of leaves, having multiple colours, typically yellow or white in addition to the usual green colour.
variety	a taxonomic rank below **species** and **subspecies**, often used to describe geographic distinctiveness in certain physical characteristics that occur naturally. In a scientific name, added after **genus** and **species** following the abbreviation 'var.' (see also **cultivar**).
vein	a vascular tissue in a leaf, carrying nutrients and usually prominently visible, their pattern helping with identification.
wood	the structural cells of a tree's stem, branches and roots, providing mechanical support and transporting nutrients. When processed is known as 'timber.'

Native trees of Britain and Ireland

↑ Elder berries.

The last glacial period (the Late Devensian) reached its maximum about 27,000 years ago, when ice covered all of Ireland and most of Britain except the south and south-east. Most trees disappeared, except low numbers of Scots Pine and willow scrub. When the ice eventually began to retreat from about 11,700 years ago, trees of other species that had survived in populations much further south in Europe (known as 'refugia') naturally began to spread north as the climate gradually warmed. Britain and Ireland were connected to mainland Europe by a land bridge ('Doggerland'), allowing tree species to spread and colonise naturally, before rising sea-levels from melting ice eventually flooded this low-lying land about 8,200 years ago.

Therefore, those tree species which naturally colonised Britain and Ireland 8,000 years ago, including those present before the last glacial period, are considered **native**. Any species arriving afterwards is likely to have been assisted by people, and whether deliberately or accidentally, is considered **non-native**.

Most conservationists stick to the principle that our semi-natural woodlands are comprised of native trees, but there are discussions about whether there should be a local, regional, national or Britain and Ireland-wide definition of nativeness. For example, European Beech is considered only native to south-east Britain. Others consider that there are 'shades of nativeness' and would include species that were previously native but have disappeared (e.g. Scots Pine was once widespread across Britain and Ireland, but is currently only considered truly native to Scotland).

There are two sub-divisions of non-native species. Long-established species are known as **archaeophytes**, introduced by humans from prehistoric times up to 1500AD. Example of archaeophytes include Common Walnut and Sweet Chestnut, both of which were introduced

to Britain by the Romans, and Strawberry-tree, thought to have been introduced to south-west Ireland about 4,000 years ago. Trees introduced to Britain and Ireland after the discovery of the New World, in about 1550AD, are not considered archaeophytes, and are known instead as **neophytes**.

Britain has a comparatively small number of native tree species compared to other European countries (about 45 excluding microspecies, which are small, genetically distinct populations within species), and Ireland has even fewer. Our nearest neighbour France has about 74 main species. There is a case for taking a purist stance about native tree species (especially when considering associated biodiversity, meaning that other wildlife has adapted over long periods of time to live in harmony with those tree species). But in the context of threats from climate change in particular, there are strong arguments for more flexibility in environmental policy and conservation practice. While 'exotic' is a helpful simple term in many ways, 'alien' is loaded with subtext and can refer to the capacity for some non-native species to become invasive.

In this guide, 'native' (to either Britain and/or Ireland) and 'non-native' (to both countries) are applied simply to define each species described, while a definition of non-native status may be added to the descriptive text where applicable, whether to define its status as an archaeophyte or neophyte, and to detail a date of introduction if known. Native status follows those of the Botanical Society of Britain and Ireland.

↓ Holly (right) and Common Hawthorn (left) frame a gateway.

Tree species native to Britain

There are thought to be about 45 tree species native to Britain – 64 if you include 'microspecies' like Bristol or Devon Whitebeam. Some, such as Dogwood or Guelder-rose, are sometimes described as 'shrubs', but for clarity and simplicity, in this book all species are considered to be trees of different shapes and forms. Note that not all native species in the list opposite are featured in this guide, with some excluded due to rarity or uncommon status (marked with *).

↓ Branches of a Goat Willow in spring covered in catkins.

Common name	Scientific name
Field Maple	Acer campestre
Common Whitebeam	Aria edulis
Round-leaved Whitebeam *	Aria eminens
Lancastrian Whitebeam *	Aria lancastriensis
Grey-leaved Whitebeam *	Aria porrigentiformis
Rock Whitebeam *	Aria rupicola
Bloody Whitebeam *	Aria vexans
Wilmott's Whitebeam *	Aria wilmottiana
Black Alder	Alnus glutinosa
Dwarf Birch *	Betula nana
Silver Birch	Betula pendula
Downy Birch	Betula pubescens
Box	Buxus sempervirens
Hornbeam	Carpinus betulus
Service-tree	Cormus domestica
Dogwood	Cornus sanguinea
Hazel	Corylus avellana
Midland Hawthorn	Crataegus laevigata
Common Hawthorn	Crataegus monogyna
Broom *	Cytisus scoparius
Spindle	Euonymus europaeus
European Beech	Fagus sylvatica
Alder Buckthorn	Frangula alnus
Common Ash	Fraxinus excelsior
Arran Whitebeam *	Hedlundia arranensis
Arran Service-tree *	Hedlundia pseudofennica
English Whitebeam *	Hedlundia anglica
Sea Buckthorn	Hippophae rhamnoides
Holly	Ilex aquifolium
Common Juniper	Juniperus communis
Bristol Whitebeam *	Karpatiosorbus bristoliensis
Devon Whitebeam *	Karpatiosorbus devoniensis
Somerset Whitebeam *	Karpatiosorbus subcuneata
Crab Apple	Malus sylvestris
Scots Pine	Pinus sylvestris
Black Poplar	Populus nigra subsp. betulifolia
Aspen	Populus tremula
Wild Cherry	Prunus avium
Bird Cherry	Prunus padus
Blackthorn	Prunus spinosa
Plymouth Pear	Pyrus cordata
Sessile Oak	Quercus petraea
Pedunculate Oak	Quercus robur
Purging Buckthorn	Rhamnus cathartica
White Willow	Salix alba
Goat Willow	Salix caprea
Grey Willow	Salix cinerea
Crack Willow	Salix fragilis
Bay Willow *	Salix pentandra
Purple Osier *	Salix purpurea
Almond Willow *	Salix triandra
Common Osier	Salix viminalis
Elder	Sambucus nigra
Rowan	Sorbus aucuparia
Yew	Taxus baccata
Small-leaved Lime	Tilia cordata
Large-leaved Lime	Tilia platyphyllos
Wild Service-tree *	Torminalis glaberrima
Common Gorse	Ulex europaeus
Western Gorse *	Ulex gallii
Wych Elm	Ulmus glabra
Field Elm	Ulmus minor agg.
Wayfaring-tree	Viburnum lantana
Guelder-rose	Viburnum opulus

Tree species native to Ireland

There are thought to be some 32 tree species native to Ireland. Only two species are considered native to Ireland yet non-native to Britain: Irish Whitebeam (*Aria hibernica*) and Strawberry-tree (*Arbutus unedo*), although the latter is contentious as some botanists now believe it is an archaeophyte. Note that not all native tree species are featured in this guide, with some excluded due to rarity or uncommon status (marked with *).

Common name	Scientific name
Black Alder	*Alnus glutinosa*
Strawberry-tree	*Arbutus unedo*
Common Whitebeam	*Aria edulis*
Irish Whitebeam *	*Aria hibernica*
Silver Birch	*Betula pendula*
Downy Birch	*Betula pubescens*
Hazel	*Corylus avellana*
Common Hawthorn	*Crataegus monogyna*
Broom *	*Cytisus scoparius*
Spindle	*Euonymus europaeus*
Alder Buckthorn	*Frangula alnus*
Common Ash	*Fraxinus excelsior*
Holly	*Ilex aquifolium*
Common Juniper	*Juniperus communis*
Crab Apple	*Malus sylvestris*
Scots Pine	*Pinus sylvestris*

Common name	Scientific name
Aspen	*Populus tremula*
Wild Cherry	*Prunus avium*
Bird Cherry	*Prunus padus*
Blackthorn	*Prunus spinosa*
Sessile Oak	*Quercus petraea*
Pedunculate Oak	*Quercus robur*
Purging Buckthorn	*Rhamnus cathartica*
Goat Willow	*Salix caprea*
Grey Willow	*Salix cinerea*
Elder	*Sambucus nigra*
Rowan	*Sorbus aucuparia*
Yew	*Taxus baccata*
Common Gorse	*Ulex europaeus*
Western Gorse *	*Ulex gallii*
Wych Elm	*Ulmus glabra*
Guelder-rose	*Viburnum opulus*

↓ A stand of Aspens in their autumn colours.

↑ An ancient Pedunculate Oak in Sherwood Forest.

Basic tree identification

Before taking your first steps in identifying a tree, it is helpful to understand some basic concepts. It may be surprising that some plants known as trees are technically not trees at all! Understanding the terms conifer and broadleaved, and evergreen and deciduous, is also very important.

What is a tree?

The simplest definition of a tree is: **a large plant with a woody stem**. All 'true' trees belong to the eudicotyledon (often shortened to 'eudicot') division of plants, meaning plants with true (eu) two (di) seed leaves (cotyledon).

Some large plants may look like trees but do not have stems of wood, even if made of a very strong plant material (for example, tightly packed leaf bases). Such plants are from another group known as a monocotyledon or simply 'monocot', meaning one seed leaf. Examples of monocots that are not true trees, some even with 'tree' in their common name, include:

- Bamboo
- Banana
- Joshua Tree
- Palm Tree

A 'shrub' is another term sometimes used to describe a small tree with multiple stems. However, it is not especially helpful because large trees (for example, Common Ash or Hornbeam) can be coppiced, making them small with multiple stems! Who's to say that a Common Juniper is a tree or shrub, or how to define a Dwarf Birch? It is much easier simply to disregard the term 'shrub' altogether, and instead to talk only of trees and then to describe their size and form.

Conifer or broadleaved

Botanically, the difference between a **conifer**, which is technically a gymnosperm, and a **broadleaf**, known as an angiosperm, is that conifers produce naked seeds in cones, while broadleaves produce seeds within the protection of an ovary, which matures to become a fruit. There are some cases that can seem confusing, for example Yew protects its seed in a fleshy aril, which has the appearance of a fruit. However, it is actually a drastically modified cone (not a swollen ovary), meaning Yew is a conifer belonging to the gymnosperms.

↓ Norway Spruce cones.

↑ Italian Alder leaves.

An easier identification aid for non-botanists is that most broadleaves have large flat leaves, while most conifers have needles or small scale-like leaves.

Maidenhair-tree (or Ginkgo) is a special exception. While it is a gymnosperm, it is not a conifer, instead being the only species belonging to the taxonomic group of Ginkgophyta. It has flat leaves and fleshy fruits borne on stalks, but is different from both conifers and broadleaves.

Deciduous or evergreen

Does the tree have green leaves all year round? If it retains living leaves for the whole year then it is **evergreen**. If its leaves die in winter then it is **deciduous**. Note that some tree species may retain foliage all through the winter even though they are dead leaves, but they are still defined as deciduous (for example, the brown, dead leaves of European Beech and Hornbeam). An interesting fact is that evergreen trees do lose their leaves but not all at once. Each leaf lasts a year or more, dying at different times to neighbouring leaves, and overall giving a conifer its evergreen appearance.

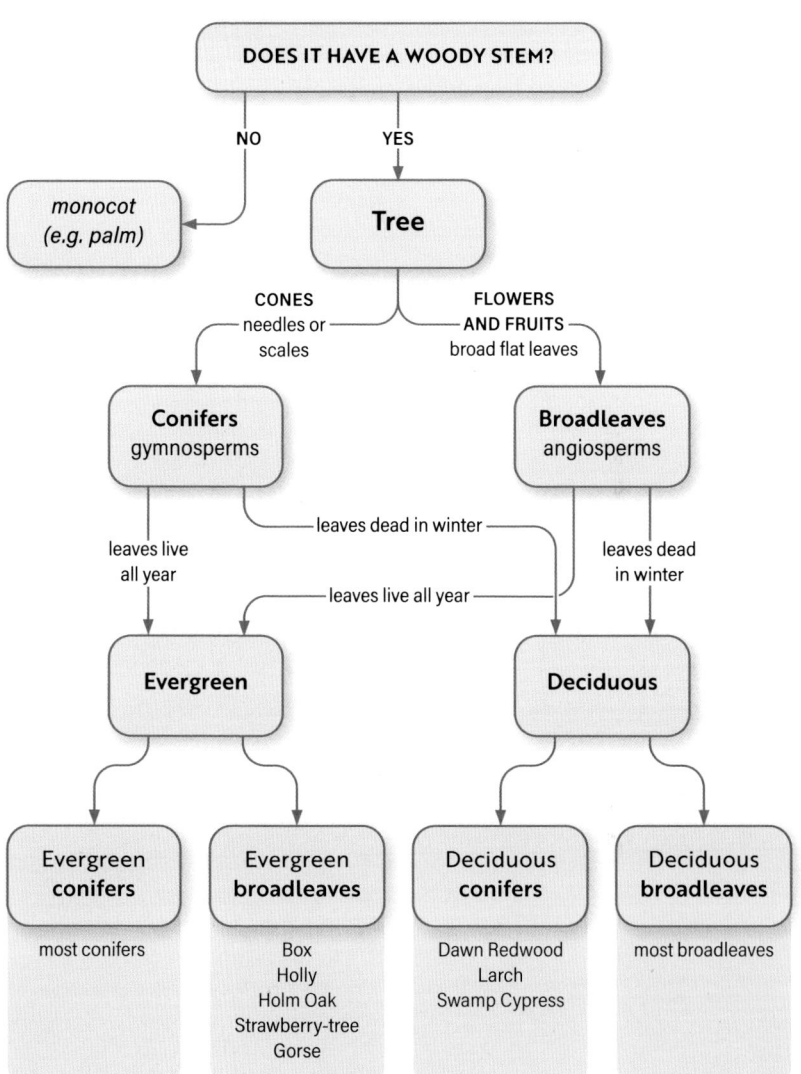

DOES IT HAVE A WOODY STEM?

NO → *monocot (e.g. palm)*

YES → **Tree**

CONES — needles or scales → **Conifers** gymnosperms

FLOWERS AND FRUITS — broad flat leaves → **Broadleaves** angiosperms

leaves live all year → **Evergreen**

leaves dead in winter

leaves live all year

leaves dead in winter → **Deciduous**

Evergreen conifers
most conifers

Evergreen broadleaves
Box
Holly
Holm Oak
Strawberry-tree
Gorse

Deciduous conifers
Dawn Redwood
Larch
Swamp Cypress

Deciduous broadleaves
most broadleaves

First steps in identifying a tree

Many people may be too quick to guess that a conifer is a 'pine' or even a 'Christmas tree', or take a wild guess that a large broadleaved tree is an oak. It is better to identify a tree at a higher level, such as whether it is an 'evergreen conifer', than to make a random guess that a tree is a 'pine', which is just as likely as not to be incorrect, as it could be a fir, spruce or cypress etc.

One of the best steps in learning to

identify a tree is to start by ascertaining whether the tree is deciduous or evergreen, and also whether it is a conifer or broadleaved, and then to combine both these elements. Following this method also means that some obvious anomalies can be ruled out, namely the few cases of evergreen broadleaves (such as Box, Holly, Holm Oak) and deciduous conifers (such as Dawn Redwood, larches, Swamp Cypress).

Next steps in identifying a tree

Once you have worked out whether a tree is a conifer or broadleaved, and deciduous or evergreen, it becomes a little more complicated. The challenge of completing identification confidently can vary through the year. For example, it can be easier when a tree is in flower or in full leaf during the summer. Equally, there can be clues in the middle of winter when parts of a tree otherwise beyond

reach fall to the ground or become visible in the crown.

Sections provided at the start of the conifer (p.37) and broadleaved (p.93) chapters provide clues helpful in identifying a tree to the level of genus, if not species. Dichotomous leaf keys are included for conifers and broadleaves. Overall tree size and shape can be helpful, while at certain times of the year, flowers or fruits/cones can be unmistakable. Bark is generally the least reliable feature for tree identification, partly as it is difficult to describe accurately and because it can be highly variable. Read the species descriptions carefully, noting that some trees are less common in some parts of Britain and Ireland, and unlikely to be found in certain soils or habitats.

→ Caucasian Wingnut.

↓ Mixed forest of European Larch and European Beech.

Basic tree identification

Woodland habitats and communities

Britain and Ireland are fortunate to have many precious natural habitats, although some are threatened by economic development, housing, agricultural practices and global climate change. In addition, Britain and Ireland are considered to be among the most nature-depleted countries in the world. Our treescapes and woodlands are therefore crucially important in protecting and conserving rare and declining wildlife from these impacts, but they can only do so if the trees remain in place and healthy.

↓ A mature Common Ash takes centre stage among scattered broadleaves in the Lake District.

Habitats

Woodland habitats are the natural wooded environments where plants, animals and other organisms live and find the resources they need to survive. Of course, trees are critically important components of a woodland habitat, not just at a large scale, such as the canopy of a woodland, but at an individual tree level (for example, as a source of dead and dying wood that provides microhabitats for whole communities of animals, fungi and other plants). Gaps and spaces are also important, such as rides, clearings and edges, where more sunlight can reach the ground, promoting ideal conditions for

flowering plants and invertebrates. Other important tree habitats include areas with scrubby vegetation (including on the coast), traditional orchards, hedgerows and wet areas.

Many woodland habitats are common in both Britain and Ireland, while some are unique to small regions. The priority woodland and tree habitats for conservation are:

- ancient woodland (known to have been present since at least 1600 in England and Wales, 1660 in Ireland and 1750 in Scotland)
- Caledonian pinewood (unique to Scotland)
- other native conifer woodland (Yew) or scrub (Juniper)
- upland woodland (for example, oak, birch or ash woodlands)
- lowland mixed broadleaved woodland
- wet woodland (for example, alder carr woodland)
- temperate rainforest (found on the western fringes of both Britain and Ireland)
- wood pasture and parkland

Plant communities

Ecologists use the term 'plant community' to describe a specific group of plant species growing naturally together in a location, often characterised by their interactions and shared environmental conditions. A plant community is therefore part of a habitat, which includes animals, fungi and other taxa. An understanding of a plant community is helpful for land managers in learning how best to care for a woodland, and to measure change over time.

In formal systems, a community is named after the dominant tree species which creates the conditions for all the plant species that grow together, and some are subdivided further into subcommunities. Examples of woodland plant communities (note that all are native species) include:

- Willow woodlands
- Downy Birch woodlands
- Alder woodlands
- Ash woodlands
- Oak woodlands (either mixed Pedunculate–Sessile, or separately)
- Beech woodlands
- Scots Pine woodlands

Biodiversity

Biodiversity means the variety of all life found in a woodland or other habitat, including animals, plants, fungi and microorganisms. It's not only the species themselves, but also the diversity of genes within a species.

Associated biodiversity is a specific category which refers to the organisms closely linked to and interacting with trees and woodlands. This relates to all taxa (meaning any taxonomic rank, whether species, genus or family etc.), among different kingdoms of plant, animal, fungus or microorganism. Associated biodiversity can include, for example, all the invertebrates dependent on a woodland habitat or individual tree species. In some cases,

some taxa may only be found in certain types of woodland, or even a specific tree species, in which case they are known as 'obligate'.

It is important to have an understanding of associated biodiversity in supporting efforts to conserve the natural world. There is so much we don't know or appreciate about nature, and we are constantly appreciating more about its wondrous complexity. For example, when dieback first began to kill ash trees across Europe during the 2010s, scientists undertook urgent research to understand the implications for associated biodiversity. They discovered that the

↓ Sessile Oak trees.

→ Red squirrels in Sessile Oak.

bark of ash is alkaline, and that this was an important feature in supporting many invertebrates, fungi and lichens (like rare Lobarian 'leafy' lichens). They were then able to look in hope to other tree species which could provide alternative similar conditions, and rather surprisingly discovered that Sycamore was often a good alternative host for many species.

Many trees fulfil a specific ecological 'niche' in that they provide the ideal conditions important for other species. The rare Purple Emperor butterfly only lives in broadleaved woodlands, especially those with mature oak trees where they feed on aphid honeydew, while its larvae feed on willow trees in the understorey or along ride edges. Box provides a nutritious elaiosome to tempt ants to help disperse its tiny seeds.

Sometimes ecological niches can be created accidentally by people. When thousands of hectares of Lodgepole Pine were planted in mid-Wales for timber production in the 1950s, none of the foresters would have imagined that their seed would one day be crucial in sustaining populations of the endangered Red Squirrel. In much longer timescales, spanning millennia, traditional woodland management techniques such as coppicing created a whole range of ecological conditions that favour certain taxa, especially invertebrates and ground vascular plants.

In this guide, each tree description includes a Biodiversity section, highlighting some of the more notable animals, plants, fungi and microorganisms associated with each species.

↓ Lichens and fungi on Downy Birch.

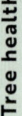

↑ Pedunculate Oak tree.

Tree health

Healthy trees equate to a healthy and resilient forest, capable of responding to changes in the environment while conserving its habitats for all the wildlife that depend on each other for survival. Sadly, in recent years there has been an ever-increasing number of pests and diseases affecting the health of our trees, both native and non-native species.

The decline in tree health is being caused by two main factors.

First, variations in the environment due to climate change, specifically milder winters and hotter summers. This affects our seasons and therefore the timing of natural events like flowering and leafing (whose study is known as phenology). Such changes create new 'spaces' for tree pests and diseases to take hold, whether they have been present for some time and not previously been a significant problem, or whether they are new pests and pathogens exploiting ideal conditions for the first time. Climate change is also stressing the environment, making trees more susceptible to a pest or disease. Also related to climate change are increases in the number of impactful events, such as drought, wildfires and extreme storms, which either stress trees or create the perfect conditions for worrying new pests and diseases. For example, windblown spruce trees create the ideal conditions for the Eight-toothed Spruce Bark Beetle, which is a serious threat to commercial forestry.

The second main factor is the global trade in plants and other goods. Many significant pests and diseases have been introduced accidentally to Britain

↑ Oak Processionary moth caterpillars nest on oak trees and feed on their leaves. Their long hairs can irritate the skin and cause respiratory issues.

→ One sign of ash dieback is dark lesions on the stem or trunk.

in combating these effects. This is not only true at a species level, but also at a genetic level (i.e. diversity within a tree species). For example, Dutch elm disease has devastated our native Field Elm populations, but mostly because these trees propagate clonally, meaning they have little genetic variation and therefore had reduced ability to adapt to the threat. On the other hand, ash dieback has proven to be a devastating pathogen, but thankfully it seems that about 5 per cent of the Common Ash population has some level of resistance.

A great deal of work is being undertaken by government authorities, the tree nursery trade, environmental non-governmental organisations (NGOs) and scientists to combat the causes of these threats and introduce actions

and Ireland, either directly on the leaves, shoots or soil of live plants, or in packaging materials. Authorities are on high alert for such pests, one of the most concerning being the Asian Longhorn Beetle. This species threatens a variety of broadleaved trees, and has already briefly been introduced in packing crates and escaped into the wild before a successful (but costly) eradication regime. Another example is the Oak Processionary moth (which is of equal concern to human health and our native oaks), introduced to Britain via its eggs on large container-grown trees imported from the near continent. It is now a serious problem in London and south-east England.

The diversity of our trees and woodland habitats is really important

to improve the health of our trees and woodlands. Individuals can also help. Volunteers can take part in various tree health initiatives; see Resources (p.236) for further information and links.

Wood

Wood is the main structural component of trees, and one of the key factors that differentiates true trees (eudicots, see p.23) from other large plants (monocots). Once wood is processed for use by people, it is known as 'timber'.

A tree stem consists of layers of different tissues. On the outside are phloem tissues, transporting food (sugars) produced by leaves during photosynthesis to other parts of the tree, while dead phloem tissues on the outside of the tree stem are collectively known as bark. Inside the phloem is a vascular layer called the cambium, separating phloem from xylem tissues. The xylem tissues transport water and minerals dissolved by the roots upwards towards the tree's leaves, flowers and fruits. The xylem is found towards the centre of a stem and makes up the main bulk of a tree stem, essentially the 'wood' of a tree. The xylem tissues undergo lignification, which naturally strengthens the cell walls, the lignin giving wood its structural strength. Trees are capable of primary and secondary growth, meaning stems and branches can thicken (grow outwards), not just elongate at shoot and root tips (primary growth).

In a monocot plant (for example, a banana 'tree') its stem is held up mostly by water pressure, with nutrients being passed up its stem via vascular bundles distributed throughout the stem, not in concentric rings as in trees because monocots don't have a vascular cambium. Some monocots, like palm and bamboo, can produce secondary growth, although it is different to that in true trees.

Initially, all the wood of a tree forms part of its sapwood. As the tree grows, the innermost wood can undergo a chemical transformation, becoming relatively inactive and resistant to

↓ A grove of Coast Redwoods, which produce softwood timber.

↑ A top-quality stand of Sycamore, managed to produce seeds for the forest industry.

decay. This is known as heartwood. The proportion of heartwood and the rate at which it is produced varies considerably between tree species. Black Locust and European Beech have thin sapwood, while in Common Walnut it can be thick (being slower to change into heartwood). In some species, there is a clear colour difference between sapwood and heartwood, as in Yew and Common Walnut.

Tree stems expand at different rates during the year, expanding more quickly in spring and early summer, before slowing and pausing growth altogether during winter months. This variable growth creates the distinctive pale (fast growth) and dark (slow growth) rings seen in a tree stem when cut open. These are the 'tree rings' that dendrochronologists count and measure to date wood. Some trees have additional ribbon-like structures radiating outwards (running perpendicular to the growth rings), known as medullary rays. Dependent on the angle of cutting, these can produce stunning ripples and other patterns in timber, much loved by furniture makers.

The commonly used terms hardwood and softwood to describe timber can be confusing. Simply, hardwood is only produced by broadleaves (angiosperms) and softwood by conifers (gymnosperms). However, the softwood produced by some conifers can be extremely 'hard' (for example, Yew), and conversely the hardwood produced by some broadleaves can be very 'soft' (for example, poplars).

Gymnosperms (conifers and Maidenhair-tree)

Gymnosperms are woody, perennial, seed-producing trees. Their name comes from the Greek meaning 'naked seed' because their seeds are not enclosed in an ovary, like those of angiosperms (p.93). Instead, their seeds develop on the scales of a cone, or sometimes in significantly modified cones which have the appearance of a fruit but are technically a different structure (for example, an 'aril' for Yew, or an exposed seed with a hard coat 'sarcotesta' for Maidenhair-tree). They produce softwood timber, as opposed to the hardwood timber produced by broadleaves, although that doesn't mean it can't be hard or strong

← Emerging foliage of Dawn Redwood in spring.

(for example, Yew softwood is harder than many broadleaved hardwoods).

Conifers featured are split into four families (species included in this book are in parentheses):

- Pinaceae (true firs, true cedars, European Larch, spruces, pines, Douglas-fir, Western Hemlock)
- Taxaceae (Yew)
- Cupressaceae (Common Juniper, redwoods, red cedars, cypresses)
- Araucariaceae (Monkey Puzzle).

The Maidenhair-tree (p.91) is classified as a gymnosperm yet is not a conifer, being the sole species in the Ginkgophyta division, and in the Ginkgoaceae family.

The diversity of gymnosperms illustrated in three trees: the needles of Scots Pine (*left*), the soft spray of Lawson's Cypress (*below*) and the unique leaves of the Maidenhair-tree (*below left*).

Gymnosperm identification

Leaves, which in the case of conifers are either like needles or scales, are among the most reliable form of identification, and sometimes cones are also helpful. This simple key will help you narrow down the identity of a tree by its leaves and cones.

Definitions:
- **foliage:** deciduous or evergreen
- **leaf form:** descriptions of leaf shapes
- **leaf architecture:** the pattern by which the leaves grow on shoots
- **features to spot:** further clues to help distinguish between closely related species

Deciduous foliage

Leaf form	Leaf architecture	Features to spot	See	Page
broad	fan	fleshy-coated seeds (fruit-like), no cones	Maidenhair-tree	93
needles	flat ranks	buds and leaves alternate along shoot	Swamp Cypress	85
		buds and leaves opposite along shoot	Dawn Redwood	79
	rosettes	small upright cones, soft light green foliage	European Larch	53

Evergreen foliage

Leaf form	Leaf architecture	Features to spot	See	Page
triangular	whorls	large, leathery, triangular leaves, growing spirally	Monkey Puzzle	69
		small, sharp-pointed scales, growing spirally	Japanese Red Cedar	73
needles	bundled in pairs	grey-green twisted needles (15cm), terminal bud blunt	Corsican Pine	61
		mid-green twisted needles (10cm), terminal bud blunt, cone scales have a slight prickle	Lodgepole Pine	59
		blue-green twisted needles (7cm), terminal bud blunt	Scots Pine	63
	flat ranks	needles grow on side shoots, but main shoots have scale-like leaves	Coast Redwood	81
		female cones are red arils	Yew	89
		upright cones, needles grow from a sucker-like pad, silver underside with notched tip	European Silver Fir	41

Cones can be a useful point of differentiation between different conifers. Compare the cones of Norway Spruce (*left*), Lodgepole Pine (*centre*) and Western Red Cedar (*right*).

Evergreen foliage (continued)

Leaf form	Leaf architecture	Features to spot	See	Page
(needles continued)	(flat ranks continued)	upright cones, needles grow from a sucker-like pad, narrow white bands underneath, tip unnotched, citrus scent	Grand Fir	43
		upright cones, needles grow from a sucker-like pad, blue-green, green-grey underside, upward curving, rounded tips, onion scent	Noble Fir	45
		drooping globular cones, citrus-scented foliage	Western Hemlock	67
	rosettes	branches ascend	Atlas Cedar	47
		branches level	Cedar of Lebanon	51
		branches descend	Deodar	49
	bottle brush	hanging cones, needle can be rolled between finger and thumb	Norway Spruce	55
		hanging cones, impossible to roll a needle between finger and thumb	Sitka Spruce	57
		hanging cones (three-pronged bracts stick out between scales), needles soft, flexible and aromatic	Douglas-fir	65
scales	flat ferny spray	globular cones droop, parsley-scented foliage	Lawson's Cypress	71
		upright flask-shaped cones, sweet aromatic foliage	Western Red Cedar	87
	rounded spray	acrid-smelling foliage, flattened towards tips	Leyland Cypress	75
		fine, sharp tips to leaves	Giant Redwood	83
	whorls	blue-green foliage, in whorls of three	Common Juniper	77

European Silver Fir *Abies alba*

Native to the mountain ranges of central and eastern Europe, this attractive true fir was introduced to Britain in 1603. Specimens can grow to 50m or more in height, with a trunk girth of 9m.

Biology This is a true mountain species, thriving in the Pyrenees, Alps and the Carpathian Mountains. Monoecious, with female cones in the upper canopy. Cones and seeds are produced after about 25 years old. Seedlings naturally regenerate freely yet seeds can remain dormant for many years, waiting for sunlight to appear after a new gap opens up in the forest canopy. Trees can live 500 years or more.

Identification Bark silver-grey, split into squarish plates, while stem often retains branch stubs. The underside of its 2–3cm needles are a silvery white underneath with a tiny notch at their tips and grow quite flattened along a branch. Long cones with bracts which protrude between scales, usually high in canopy and disintegrate on the tree, meaning they do not assist much with identification. *Compare with Grand Fir (p.43): needles longer and more flattened.*

Culture Quite a slow-growing tree. Seedlings sensitive to frost. Very tolerant of shade, capable of growing underneath older trees. Prefers well-drained soils, and dislikes urban pollution or salt-laden sea winds. Foresters like to plant it in mixtures with other species.

Biodiversity Often found growing with European Beech and other broadleaves in its natural range, its evergreen canopy providing shelter for birds and mammals, especially in winter.

Threats Prone to aphids, bark beetle pests and fungal pathogens, and very sensitive to fire. Unlikely to thrive under a warming climate.

Stem of European Silver Fir. Notice the branch stubs.

Male cones (strobili).

Foliage.

Grand Fir   *Abies grandis*

A very tall and majestic species of true fir, native to the western coastal areas of North America. Introduced to Britain in 1831 by Victorian plant hunter David Douglas.

Biology Two distinct varieties of this species can be found in its native range; one in coastal areas (e.g. Cascade Mountains), the other further inland. The former thrives better in Britain and Ireland. Monoecious, with female cones in the upper canopy. Seeds produced from cones on older trees.

Identification Among the most vigorous of the true firs, growing to 60m or more in height. Bark silver, cracking into rectangular plates. Foliage has an attractive tangy citrus smell. Needles 25–50mm grow flat on either side of a shoot, their underside with narrow white bands, and notched tips. Cones small (8–10cm) with no visible bracts. *Compare with European Silver Fir (p.41): notched needles, shorter and less flattened on shoot, cone bracts extend beyond scales.*

Culture Grows best in humid areas with high rainfall. Dislikes exposure, especially to sea winds. Moderately tolerant of shade. One of the most productive timber trees. Can be grown in mixtures with other tree species. Popular as a Christmas tree in North America.

Biodiversity Provides shelter to birds and mammals in its native range, and natural recovery after wildfires.

Threats Intolerant of drought, which causes mortality in seedlings, and in mature trees, splits in trunks and timber. Flammable foliage and tendency to hold branches low down makes it fire-prone.

Stem of a mature Grand Fir. Notice the branch stubs in whorls.

Old needles with young growth emerging.

Young cones.

Noble Fir *Abies procera*

The largest true fir, relatively uncommon in the forests of Britain and Ireland where it was introduced in 1830. More likely to be seen in parks and large gardens where, despite its size, it sways majestically in the strongest of gales.

Biology Native to Washington and Oregon in North America. Grows up to high altitudes and along exposed ridges. Monoecious, with female cones in the upper canopy. Large and heavy cones produced on mature trees.

Identification Bark silver-grey with long fissures, and trunk tapers very little for full height of tree (60m). Blue-green, aromatic foliage grows densely along shoots, particularly at tips, where like a bottle brush. Needles tend to curl upwards and have rounded tips, with two green-grey stripes on underside.

Culture Fast-growing, very windfirm, moderately shade-tolerant (less than other true firs), but fire-prone. Thrives best in moist western regions of Britain and Ireland. Timber good quality, light and strong (once used in aeroplane construction), but not durable. A popular Christmas tree due to dense foliage and smell.

Biodiversity A hardy species that grows where many other conifers struggle, and can regenerate prolifically after fire or other major disturbances. Seeds and seedlings survived Mount St Helens volcanic eruption in 1980, protected by a blanket of snow.

Threats Relatively free from serious pests or pathogens. A warming climate will restrict its range further in Britain and Ireland.

Young foliage of Noble Fir is a brighter green.

Male cones (strobili).

Silver-grey, fissured bark of Noble Fir.

Blue-green mature foliage.

Noble Fir – Gymnosperms

Atlas Cedar *Cedrus atlantica*

Native to the Atlas and Rif Mountains of North Africa, introduced to Britain and Ireland in about 1844, but first catalogued by botanists in 1827.

Biology Grows up to 2,000m altitude in its native range, often on rocky soils, exposed to heavy winter snowfall and hot, dry summers. Thrives in mixed forests of conifers and broadleaves, reaching a height of 40m. Monoecious, male cones 3–4cm, falling after releasing pollen. Female cones 8–12cm long, maturing after two years when they become woody (cones dimpled at tip), releasing a winged seed.

Identification Distinguishing between the true cedars is never easy, but generally the following holds true for branching habit: ascending – Atlas; level – Lebanon (p.51); descending – Deodar (p.49). Atlas Cedar has less prominent 'plates' of foliage than other true cedars. Needles 20mm and quite stiff, growing in rosettes. All true cedar species grow needles in rosettes, like European Larch (p.53), but are not deciduous. Cones growing erect on cedar branches can help distinguish from many other conifers.

Culture Grow in well-drained soil, and avoid areas with high rainfall. Hardy to –20°C. Not very shade-tolerant, so provide plenty of light. Makes a superb specimen tree for a large garden. Highly durable timber with lovely fragrance.

Biodiversity In their native range, forests with Atlas Cedar provide habitat for the endangered Barbary Macaque.

Threats Considered endangered in its native range due to exploitation. Also increasingly impacted by drought.

Ascending branches of Atlas Cedar.

Immature cone among foliage.

Bark.

Deodar *Cedrus deodara*

Deodara means 'tree of the gods', and this majestic true cedar is sacred to Hindus, introduced in 1831. Its durable timber was once favoured for shipbuilding.

Biology Unlike the other two true cedars featured, which are Mediterranean in origin, Deodar is native to the Western Himalayas, including India and Pakistan (where it is the national tree). Monoecious, wind-pollinated.

Identification Foliage grows in 'plates' on branches which usually descend on mature trees. Often a single straight trunk. *Compare branches: level with Cedar of Lebanon (p.51), and ascending with Atlas Cedar (p.47).* Look for drooping leader, and foliage often visibly more green than other true cedars. Needles quite soft, up to 50mm long. Large female (seed) cones grow upright on branches, cone tips flat-topped.

Culture Grow in sheltered and well-drained sites, avoiding clay and alkaline soils. Water young trees during periods of drought. Later, little care needed. Specimen trees need lots of room, so avoid tight spaces. Can be grown in mixed forests, kept free of competition from neighbouring trees, although their shade can reduce heavy branching, which Deodar can be prone to.

Biodiversity In its native range, grows in mixed forests of maples, oaks, true firs, junipers and pines.

Threats Generally problem free, but like many conifers can be infected by honey fungus. May benefit by a warming climate, resisting drought conditions.

Soft foliage of Deodar.

Bark of a mature tree.

Remains of a cone on the forest floor.

Male cone (strobili) and foliage.

Cedar of Lebanon *Cedrus libani*

A majestic species with deep cultural significance, including in various religions, and featuring in the national flag of Lebanon. Produces rich brown-coloured and aromatic timber.

Biology Native to Asia Minor and occurring naturally in mixed conifer forests in Lebanon, Syria, and eastern Mediterranean countries. Introduced to Britain and Ireland in the seventeenth century, if not earlier. Monoecious, wind-pollinated.

Identification A majestic tree growing to 35m tall with dark green level 'plates' of foliage, although easily confused with other true cedars. Barrel-shaped cones have sunken tops. They grow vertically from shoots, and disintegrate on branches.

Culture Most often grown in the open as a specimen tree in parks and large gardens, though also grows well in woodland where it can become quite vigorous unless shaded. Hardy to extreme cold but dislikes wet ground. Prone to sudden dropping of its substantial branches, so needs careful management.

Biodiversity Invertebrates find homes in its bark crevices, while trunk hollows created after large branch drops create roosting and nesting sites for bats and owls.

Threats Threatened in its native range by advances in agriculture. Likely to thrive in a warmer and drier climate in future, being quite resistant to drought. Few pests or pathogens.

Foliage.

Mature cones, beginning to disintegrate.

Bark.

European Larch *Larix decidua*

Unusual in being a conifer that loses its foliage in winter (deciduous), European Larch is an elegant, fast-growing tree that produces valuable timber for use in construction.

Biology The only deciduous conifer native to Europe, probably introduced to Britain in the late sixteenth century. Monoecious, female flowers (later cones) a pretty deep ruby colour, appearing among bright green emerging needles in spring, growing on the same tree as the unremarkable male cones.

Identification Deciduous conifer is a key identification feature: *in winter, compare with Maidenhair-tree (p.93), Swamp Cypress (p.85) and Dawn Redwood (p.79).* Needles grow in clusters, like true cedars (which are evergreen). Fine sprays of soft needles hang elegantly below branches. Foliage turns attractive yellow before falling in autumn. Cones, upright on shoots, are important in differentiating between different larch species: European Larch has straight scales, while on Japanese Larch they curl backwards so cones appear like rosettes. Note the two species also hybridise.

Culture Grows well at high altitudes, preferring well-drained soils with shelter. Intolerant of sea winds and urban pollution. A pioneer species, establishing easily after planting. Attractive in the landscape, especially woodland edges. A good companion tree for valuable hardwood species like oak. Larch hybrids were once popular in forestry, as trees are very vigorous.

Biodiversity Seeds attract birds and Red Squirrels.

Threats Sadly, prone to several diseases and pathogens, particularly *Phytophthora ramorum*, limiting its planting.

Bright green spring foliage with mature female cones.

Cones are retained through the winter, remaining upright.

Young female cones in early spring.

European Larch – Gymnosperms

53

Norway Spruce *Picea abies*

A tough conifer, at home in mountains and tundra. Native to mainland Europe but introduced sometime before the sixteenth century. The original Christmas tree in Britain and Ireland, it produces valuable lightweight softwood when mature.

Biology Monoecious, small cream-coloured male cones producing copious pollen in spring, on the same tree as female cones. When mature, elegant long female cones release seed, though often infertile in Britain and Ireland.

Identification Typically grows tall (up to 50m) and tapered like a spire, except in old trees when more rounded. Branches bear needles on small 'pegs' (pulvini), each sharp green, slightly curved and square in cross-section, making it possible to roll them between finger and thumb. Bark scaly and cracked, red-brown. Cones hang from branches, up to 20cm long with papery scales. *Compare with Sitka Spruce (p.57): bark without red hue, shorter cones, needles straight and diamond in cross-section and impossible to roll between fingers.*

Culture Prefers moist soils, even tolerating waterlogging. Able to thrive under light shade, so suitable in mixed forests. Grows slowly at first, but then vigorous. Low fertility limits natural regeneration.

Biodiversity Provides shelter to wildlife all year round. Its seeds are favourite food of Red Squirrel. Foliage eaten by larvae of several moth species.

Threats Prone to root rot and honey fungus. Also Eight-toothed Spruce Bark Beetle.

Mature female (seed) cones.

Bark.

Immature female cone.

Foliage.

Sitka Spruce *Picea sitchensis*

Native to the Pacific coast of North America and introduced in 1831, this species became the principal commercial timber species during large-scale afforestation of the uplands in the twentieth century.

Biology At home in wet, humid and harsh environments. Monoecious, producing male and female cones on the same tree when at least 30 years old.

Identification Growing to 60m tall with a long leader. Its sharp, spiny, dark green needles are a flattened diamond in cross-section, with two bright bands on the underside. Cones hang below branches, up to 10cm long. Bark is purple-grey with scaly plates. *Compare with Norway Spruce (p.55).*

Culture Grows best in the wet uplands of Britain and Ireland. For timber production, clones of the most suitable provenances (origins) are recommended. Branches grow very densely, so if not brashed (side-pruned), plantations become impenetrable.

Biodiversity Dense monocultures of Sitka Spruce prevent any ground flora growing beneath their canopies. However, well-managed plantations shelter large mammals, and provide seeds for small birds including crossbills and nesting sites for birds of prey.

Threats Generally healthy, but impacted by aphids and spruce bark beetles.

Scaly bark plates.

Male cones (strobili).

Sitka Spruce plantation.

Sitka Spruce – Gymnosperms

57

Lodgepole Pine *Pinus contorta* subsp. *latifolia*

Introduced in 1853 from the Pacific coast of North America, this tough species grows where few other trees dare, thriving in exposed and wet uplands.

Biology An inland subspecies of Shore Pine. In its native range, often highly effective at recolonising after a wildfire. Monoecious.

Identification All three featured pine species grow needles in pairs, but other pine species have needles bundled in threes or fives. Site is useful for identification as the three pines grow in different places; Lodgepole favours harsh and wet conditions. Needles 6–10cm, mid-green and twisted, terminal bud long and blunt. Slender cones to 5cm, slight prickle on scales. Bark has dull brown-black, quite flaky square plates. *Compare with Scots Pine (p.63): needles darker green, bark reddish hue and less flaky. Compare with Corsican*

Pine (p.61): dry sites, terminal bud broad with sudden point.

Culture Grows in exposed, waterlogged and cold sites. Also tolerant of salt, so can be found near the coast or snowy roads routinely treated in winter. Important to choose the best provenance (origin) of seed for growing in Britain and Ireland.

Biodiversity No specific species are associated, although plantations have sustained populations of Red Squirrel in Wales. Provides shelter and nesting sites to birds and mammals in exposed places. Can be invasive in Caledonian pinewoods.

Threats Red-band needle blight affects trees, particularly when grown densely together.

Mature female cone.

Male cones (strobili) and paired needles.

A young stem. Note whorled branches.

Corsican Pine   *Pinus nigra* subsp. *laricio*

Native to mountainous areas of the Mediterranean, including Corsica, Sicily and southern Italian mainland, it was Introduced to Britain in the late eighteenth century. Although widely planted in dry areas of eastern England for timber, it makes a grand specimen tree in a sheltered garden or park.

Biology A subspecies of Austrian or Black Pine, this is an effective pioneer tree in its native range. Monoecious, mature trees produce seed crops every three to five years.

Identification Mostly found growing in plantations on dry sites in lowland Britain, especially east (e.g. Thetford Forest) and south-east. Needles grow in pairs, grey-green, 15cm long, twisted, and flexible, terminal bud broad with sudden point. Cones 8cm and grey-brown. Bark greyish, with wide fissures. Stem usually straight and unforked.

Culture Dislikes chalky soils, thriving in dry and sandy conditions. Young trees can be difficult to establish due to intolerance to drying out (use cell-grown trees) and being frost-sensitive (avoid planting in cold spots).

Biodiversity Not highly valuable for wildlife, but provides a seed source for some birds and mammals.

Threats Red-band needle blight affects trees, causing severe needle-drop, particularly when trees are grown densely together. Resistant to urban pollution and might thrive under climate change if pest/pathogen threats controlled.

Grey, fissured bark.

Needles in pairs.

Mature cone and foliage.

Scots Pine *Pinus sylvestris*

Our only native pine is iconic in Caledonian pinewoods, but can be found growing across Britain and Ireland. Once favoured as a timber for shipbuilding, 'granny' pines are now valued in our wild landscapes and for their support of rare wildlife.

Biology Scots Pine is a pioneer, effective at colonising bare ground. One of only three conifers native to Britain (see also Juniper p.77, and Yew p.89). Monoecious, male and female flowers (cones) are produced in early summer on the same tree from about 20 years old.

Identification Bark red-grey, generally brighter red higher up stem and along branches. Needles blue-green in pairs, up to 7cm and commonly twisted, terminal bud long and blunt. Female cones 5–8cm long and woody. *Compare with Corsican Pine (p.61): long and grey-green needles, terminal bud broad with sudden point.*

Culture Easy to grow from seed but liked by browsing mammals. Dislikes wet and boggy ground. Can grow to 35m tall in plantations, where it is a good companion for broadleaves, but more commonly seen open-grown, when more rounded in shape, more heavily branched and less tall.

Biodiversity Key species in native pinewoods in Scotland, providing food and shelter for iconic species including Wildcat, Pine Marten, crossbills and Capercaillie. Also seen growing on wildlife-rich lowland heaths.

Threats Browsing deer threaten Caledonian pinewoods. Generally a healthy species, although climate change may favour the spread of new pests and pathogens.

Red-grey bark.

Foliage and mature female cones.

Male cones (strobili).

Douglas-fir *Pseudotsuga menziesii*

Before logging, Douglas-fir trees were among the world's tallest in the old growth forests along Pacific coastal regions of North America. Introduced in 1827 and valued for its very strong timber.

Biology Not a true fir (see *Abies* spp., p.40–45), but one of about six or seven species (botanists currently disagree) in a genus whose scientific name means 'hemlock-like'. Monoecious, with cones of both sexes produced on the same tree in April, the seed maturing in September.

Identification Grows up to 60m, usually in a forest among other conifers, very straight and impressive trunk. Foliage soft and flexible needles, about 3cm long, and aromatic. Female cones have distinctive three-pronged bracts extending beyond scales. Bark grey, developing large fissures with age, often with orange hue and easily recognisable with practice.

Culture Trees originating from low elevations in coastal Washington State thrive best in Britain and Ireland. Grows best in moist conditions with deep, fertile soils in western areas. Dislikes waterlogged soils and frost pockets. One of the most productive forest species, but casts a heavy shade so not a good companion for other species.

Biodiversity Supports general wildlife, but heavy shade-casting and acidifying effect in soils reduce ground flora.

Threats Productivity likely only to increase with climate change, and it is among the most resistant of species to wildfire. Susceptible to fungus-like pathogen *Phytophthora pluvialis*.

Bark showing pruned branch.

Foliage and male cones (strobili).

Mature female cones. Note the protruding three-pronged bracts.

Western Hemlock *Tsuga heterophylla*

A very graceful conifer with aromatic foliage, introduced in 1853 from the Pacific coast of North America.

Biology In the temperate rainforests of its native range it is a climax species, often growing alongside Sitka Spruce (p.57) or Douglas-fir (p.65). Monoecious, trees producing male and female cones on the same tree in spring, female seed maturing in autumn. Fallen trees create 'nurse logs', providing a nursery for regenerating seedlings.

Identification Dark green needles flattened, with finely serrated margins and quite bluntly tipped, appearing as two ranks along either side of the shoot. Foliage has a citrus smell. The leading shoot and branch tips droop. Small cones (2–3cm), pendulous, falling when brown, often covering the ground below.

Culture It is a deeply shade-tolerant species, happily biding its time in the understorey until a gap appears in the canopy, when it will grow rapidly. Needs a moist climate, and thrives best in deep and fertile soils. More prone than most conifers to drought, frost and pollution. Thin bark easily damaged. Grows very well in mixture with other species.

Biodiversity Not high conservation value, although can help diversify monoculture plantations of other conifer species.

Threats Generally free from pests or pathogens, but susceptible to conifer root and butt rot. Threatened in its native range by a pest introduced from Asia.

Foliage.

Naturally regenerating seedling on a nurse log.

Bark brown and thin.

Mature female cones.

Monkey Puzzle *Araucaria araucana*

Originating on the slopes of dormant volcanoes in the Andes Mountains, this unique tree was a sensation when imported in 1795. A 'living fossil' species, it was probably a major food source for dinosaurs during the Jurassic period (at least 150 million years ago).

Biology Usually dioecious, with separate male and female trees. Trees are wind-pollinated. Large (15cm) female cones ripen on branch tips and drop their seeds (similar to large pine nuts). In its native range, one of the first trees to grow after a wildfire.

Identification The appearance of this tree is unmistakable, with spirally arranged triangular scale-like leaves, which are large (4cm) and leathery, with sharp edges. Common in large gardens and parks. Trunk grows very straight and unforked, with live branches restricted to upper half, thought to be an adaptation to limit browsing by *Diplodocus* and other sauropods.

Culture Quite simple to grow from seed. Plant in a sheltered position in full sun. Trees require little pruning. One of few conifers that can regenerate from old wood, e.g. after storm damage.

Biodiversity In Argentina and Chile, many birds and insects are linked to this tree. In Britain and Ireland, its seeds are liked by Jays and Grey Squirrels.

Threats Logging, wildfires and clearance for livestock grazing have decimated Monkey Puzzle forests in South America. There is now greater genetic diversity in Europe's botanic collections.

Spirally arranged, triangular leaves.

Young tree.

Young stem.

Mature stem.

Lawson's Cypress *Chamaecyparis lawsoniana*

Although known as Port Orford Cedar in the timber trade, it is a member of the cypress family, native to Oregon and California in the US. Sometimes called Lawson Cypress.

Biology A monoecious conifer. There are many variants with different forms and colours, popular as garden ornamental trees.

Identification Tree leader droops. Fern-like flat foliage, leaves quite pointed but not sharp to touch. Pleasant fragrance when crushed, like parsley. Monoecious, male flowers crimson on leaf tips. Globular, small (1cm) female cones which droop slightly on the branch. Bark red-brown and spongy. *Compare with Western Red Cedar (p.87): sweet and fruity aroma of foliage, and upright flask-shaped cones. Compare with Leyland Cypress (p.75): leader does not droop, foliage has acrid resinous smell.*

Culture Grows best in moist but not waterlogged soils. Can be damaged by frost, leading to forking, and palatable to deer. It is an effective natural coloniser, and capable of growing in deep shade underneath mature conifers. An attractive landscape tree.

Biodiversity Not high conservation value, although can help diversify monoculture plantations of other conifer species, or provide diversity and year-round shelter in European Beech plantations.

Threats Brown foliage indicates an infection of *Phytophthora lateralis*, which is a serious pathogen in the tree's native range.

Flat foliage, with mature female cones.

Immature cones.

Brown spongy bark with vertical ridges.

Japanese Red Cedar *Cryptomeria japonica*

Known as Sugi in Japan, where this majestic tree grows naturally in mountain regions, it provided timber used in the construction of the country's ancient temples. Sometimes simply 'Japanese Cedar'.

Biology The only species in its genus (not closely related to Western Red Cedar p.87). Long-lived (1,000 years or even older), monoecious. Produces copious pollen (and is a major problem for hayfever sufferers).

Identification Grows up to 60m tall with a straight stem, sometimes with burrs and lignotubers at base. Bark red-brown and ridged, with fibrous strings. Small (1–2cm) scale-like leaves grow spirally, covering the stems entirely, quite sharply pointed. Monoecious, male cones small and numerous along shoot, almost sessile in the axil of a leaf near the growing tip, while female cones are globular (2cm), on the tips of branchlets. *Compare with Giant Redwood (p.38):*

leaves shorter, cones larger, bark thicker and more spongy, foliage less spiky.

Culture Dislikes exposure, preferring well-drained soils in sheltered warm sites. Shade-tolerant, so can suit being grown in mixtures with other tree species. Unusually for a conifer, can regenerate from old wood so can be coppiced. Quite vigorous growth, reaching 60m or taller, producing fragrant and very durable timber. A major commercial forestry species in Japan.

Biodiversity A food plant for endemic moth species in Japan. No special benefits where introduced, but could help diversify structure of monocultures of other conifers.

Threats Susceptible to *Phytophthora* and honey fungus.

Fibrous, red-brown bark.

Mature female (seed) cone.

Foliage.

Leyland Cypress *Cupressus × Hesperotropsis leylandii*

Leyland Cypress is an extremely tough and fast-growing tree. Its ubiquitous and often irresponsible use as a hedging plant in suburban gardens has led to a bad reputation.

Biology It is a natural hybrid between two cypress species, Monterey and Nootka. Although both parent species are non-native, Leyland Cypress first occurred naturally in Wales in 1888, so in one sense it might be considered native! It infrequently flowers and produces small (2cm) brown cones.

Identification Leader does not droop. Fern-like foliage is three-dimensional, except at tips, and has acrid resinous smell when crushed. Cones uncommon, upright, globular (2cm). *Compare with Lawson's Cypress (p.71).*

Culture Most hybrid species grow vigorously, and Leyland Cypress is no exception. It is also cold-hardy and will grow in most soils. Trees are mostly produced in nurseries as clones. Hedge trees should be trimmed regularly to avoid excessive growth. It is rarely seen in a forest but can grow well, reaching 35m in height, although usually multi-stemmed. Its timber is potentially quite useful but difficult to process due to tree form.

Biodiversity It has little to offer biodiversity, except nesting sites for garden birds, while its dense shade-casting obliterates growth of other plants.

Threats Leyland Cypress has few threats, other than people cutting back too hard, which prevents regeneration. Large trees are not windfirm.

The fern-like foliage of Leyland Cypress.

Mature cones.

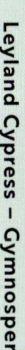

Common Juniper *Juniperus communis*

One of three conifers native to Britain and Ireland, Juniper is perhaps best known for its fragrant cones, providing flavour for gin, yet its hardy nature means it also supports important wildlife in our uplands.

Biology Grows up to 8m in sheltered locations, but can be small and prostrate when exposed and at high altitudes, where it can grow up to the tree line. Typically dioecious (occasionally monoecious). Seeds on female trees are produced in threes within berry-like cones made of three fused scales, taking two to four years to mature, becoming progressively darker. Birds ingest cones and deposit seeds in their droppings.

Identification Trees often have cones of different maturity, from green to purple-black, on the same tree. Dense blue-green foliage is prickly with a citrus scent, needles growing in whorls of three around shoots.

Culture A slow-growing and long-lived tree, perhaps 1,000 years or more. Rarely planted except in the wild. Does not thrive in shade, so normally seen in open ground and clearings.

Biodiversity In Caledonian pinewoods, Juniper helps in the transition of open ground to woodland, providing protection for Downy Birch (p.125), Rowan (p.167) and Scots Pine (p.63) seedlings, while also sheltering Black Grouse. Further south, on limestone pavements, often associated with shade-tolerant flowering plants and ferns. Cones sustain thrushes and other birds.

Threats Already vulnerable to grazing, Juniper across Britain and Ireland is now threatened by the deadly fungus-like pathogen *Phytophthora austrocedri*.

Berry-like female (seed) cones.

Red-brown bark and immature cones.

Bark tinged green by lichens.

Dawn Redwood *Metasequoia glyptostroboides*

Once thought extinct, with fossil records of this tree found in North America, a living specimen was discovered growing in China in 1941.

Biology One of few deciduous conifers. Monoecious. Rarely flowers in Britain and Ireland, but elsewhere slow to produce cones (25 years old or more).

Identification Grows to 30m tall, nearly always with a single stem. Rarely seen outside parks and large gardens where often planted near ponds and streams. Leafless branches are key feature in winter. Buds and shoots grow in opposite pairs. Bright green feathery foliage turns rich copper-red in autumn. Bark has reddish hue and spongy texture. *Compare with Swamp Cypress (p.85): winter buds and summer shoots grow alternately, bark less spongy.*

Culture Although unlikely to produce seed in Britain and Ireland, it is very easy to propagate by taking cuttings. Grows best in sheltered sites, preferring deep and moist soils. Withstands urban pollution.

Biodiversity No special wildlife is associated with this species. In its native range, often grows with mixed broadleaves that are also tolerant of wet soils.

Threats Once threatened locally by harvesting for timber, it is protected in China, and now widely propagated around the world.

Bark and foliage.

Feathery foliage.

Spongy red-brown bark.

Coast Redwood *Sequoia sempervirens*

Found growing naturally in moist coastal regions of the western US, this is the world's tallest-growing tree. Introduced in 1843, and now thrives in our oceanic climate.

Biology A monoecious conifer whose small cones can produce seed after just 15 years, but not fertile until much older. It can regenerate vegetatively as clones (suckers) emerging from its wide-spreading roots, or regrow, often as multiple trees, when blown over.

Identification Very large, impressive tree (to 50m). Rich brown to orange-coloured bark, spongy to touch. Needles grow flat along its side shoots, quite soft with two white bands beneath, while main shoots have scale-like leaves *Compare with Yew (p.89): needles taper towards tips, grey-green undersides. Compare with Giant Redwood (p.83): heavier branches, denser foliage, trunk more tapered and less likely multi-stemmed.*

Culture Unusually among conifers, it regenerates readily after being browsed by deer when young, and when cut or coppiced when mature. After a forest fire, it regrows shoots from buds buried deep in its thick, spongy bark.

Biodiversity Old trees can have multiple leaders and forks that hold pools of water, supporting a huge variety of wildlife. Its huge branches provide platforms for nesting birds.

Threats It has few pests or pathogens in its native range, where the biggest threat is logging. Root rot and honey fungus can cause root or stem breakages. Could thrive in Britain in a changing climate.

Foliage.

Orange-brown spongy bark.

Bark close-up.

Immature female (seed) cone.

Giant Redwood *Sequoiadendron giganteum*

Also known as Wellingtonia, this is a true giant, with mature specimens having the largest volume and biomass of any plant. Introduced in 1853 from California, where some specimens are more than 3,000 years old, it has since graced many parks and stately home gardens.

Biology In the Sierra Nevada, it usually dominates forest stands. It can withstand extreme wildfires, due to its thick and fibrous bark, and can regenerate from dormant buds. Monoecious, producing seeds on a two-year cycle but often retains them in its cones until triggered by stress (especially wildfire).

Identification Thick, spongy red-tinged bark on a trunk, which flares heavily at its base. Its canopy of dense blue-green foliage is born on light, curving branches. Foliage is scale-like, with fine, sharp tips. Cones small (4cm).

Culture Thrives in western regions of Britain, where the largest specimens are now more than 50m tall. Intolerant of sea winds. Grows rapidly (80cm per year). Lower branches gradually die but tend to stay attached, so foresters interested in timber need to prune. A light-demanding species. Windfirm thanks to large spreading roots. Isolated trees are often struck by lightning.

Biodiversity Outside of its native range, it has low value for biodiversity.

Threats Considered endangered in its native range. Otherwise, where introduced, generally free of diseases and pests.

Base of mature tree showing fluting.

Immature female (seed) cones.

Foliage with male cones (strobili).

Swamp Cypress *Taxodium distichum*

One of few deciduous conifers, known as the 'Bald Cypress' in the US, this tree is capable of growing in waterlogged soils. Its timber is very durable and useful in making outdoor furniture. Introduced in 1640.

Biology A monoecious conifer, native to the south-eastern US. Small (35mm) globular female cones disintegrate when mature, releasing 20–40 large seeds. The seeds float and can be dispersed by flowing water.

Identification On very wet sites, woody 'knees' can grow vertically from its roots, thought to increase stability, and trunks can be very fluted. Bark quite thin with stringy strands. Large pendulous male catkin-like strobili, 10–15cm long, can be prominent through winter months. Feathery foliage bright green in summer, slowly turning red-brown in autumn and often remaining on the tree well into winter. Winter buds and summer shoots grow alternately. *Compare with Dawn Redwood (p.79): buds and shoots grow in opposite pairs, bark more spongy.*

Culture While tolerant of flooding, this tree grows better in drier soils. It is very stable and hardy, capable of growing in a wide range of sites. One of few conifers that can regenerate when cut back severely. Can be very long-lived, with several specimens in the US more than 2,000 years old.

Biodiversity No special wildlife is associated with this species in Britain and Ireland, but in its native range it is an important species in wet habitats. Grey Squirrels and birds feed on its seeds.

Threats Few known issues in Britain or Ireland.

Bark.

Foliage and female cones.

Male cones hang like tassels.

Western Red Cedar *Thuja plicata*

In the Pacific forests of North America where it originates, this species was of huge importance to Indigenous peoples, its timber, bark and foliage used to make a huge variety of items, from dugout canoes to sanitary pads.

Biology Despite its name, this is a cypress, not a true cedar (see *Cedrus* spp., p.46–51). Monoecious, bearing male and female flowers on the same tree, the female cones produced in clusters on short stalks towards the tips of branches. In its native range this is a long-lived species, exceeding 1,000 years old.

Identification Its species name *plicata* means 'folded', referring to the origami-like folds of its dark green scale-like leaves, which are sweetly aromatic. Cones small, upright and flask-shaped. Trunk often wide and heavily buttressed at its base, bark dark red and fibrous. *Compare with Lawson's Cypress (p.71).*

Culture Thrives in areas with high rainfall, but dislikes exposed sites at higher elevations (above 200m altitude). Tolerates heavy and waterlogged soils. Quite sensitive to drought. Its narrow crown and relatively slow growth make it a good companion with broadleaves in a forest. Slow-grown trees produce durable timber which are cleft to make 'cedar' shingles.

Biodiversity Although an important species in its native range, it only supports general wildlife where introduced, providing all-year-round shelter and nesting sites.

Threats Vulnerable to honey fungus and root rot.

A mature stem showing some fluting.

Foliage with mature female (seed) cones.

Yew *Taxus baccata*

One of three native conifers, Yew has long-lasting spiritual and cultural associations, hence its common occurrence in churchyards.

Biology Trees can survive for 2,000 years or more. Yew is dioecious (separate male and female trees). Male flowers release pale pollen in spring, covering foliage. Seeds are born in distinctive berry-like red arils, distributed by feeding birds in their droppings.

Identification Dark green foliage in a broad spreading canopy with upward sweeping branches. Needles quite broad and soft, arrange horizontally on branches. Bark scaly, often with attractive hues of brown, grey and red. Female trees bear red arils.

Culture Can be grown from seeds and cuttings. Once the material of choice for longbows, its non-resinous timber is beloved by furniture makers. Foliage clippings are used in manufacture of a cancer drug. Most parts are poisonous, and trees were historically heavily cleared to protect grazing livestock. Can be planted in an understorey but will eventually dominate a woodland. A fastigiate (narrow and erect) cultivar known as Irish Yew is commonly grown in gardens.

Biodiversity Yew often dominates a woodland, casting a heavy shade which deters other plants. Provides all-year-round shelter for wildlife. Many birds, especially thrushes, enjoy its fruit.

Threats Generally free of pests and diseases.

Red, fleshy arils, containing highly toxic seeds.

Foliage and male cones (strobili). Notice the pollen dusting the surface of the leaves.

Maidenhair-tree *Ginkgo biloba*

Now rare in its native China, this elegant tree was introduced in 1758. The Maidenhair-tree or Ginkgo (sometimes misspelt 'gingko', as this resembles its pronunciation) is the only species in the Ginkgophyta division of the Gymnospermae (mostly conifers). It thrived in the Jurassic period about 170 million years ago and is considered a living fossil species. Extracts from its leaves have long been used as a herbal medicine.

Biology Separate male and female trees (dioecious). Male catkins are rarely seen in Britain and Ireland. Fertilisation occurs with motile sperm, as in ferns and mosses. Green, plum-like fleshy seeds turn yellow when ripe but have a rancid smell. Can reproduce vegetatively, including via aerial roots and suckers.

Identification Growth occurs on short spurs and appears haphazard, often from leaning and multi-stemmed trunks. Its unique fan-shaped leaves make identification easy when in leaf, but as a deciduous tree its leaves turn golden-yellow before falling (often very quickly) in autumn. When leaf-free, similar to Common Pear but has pale brown-grey and corky bark.

Culture A little frost-sensitive but will usually regenerate after damage. Light-demanding. Thrives in warm, sunny places with moderate rainfall, ideally in well-drained soils yet also grows well in rocky places. It is a very resilient species, tolerant of urban pollution, while specimens survived the fire storm caused by the atomic bomb dropped on Hiroshima during the Second World War.

Biodiversity Grows among mixed broadleaves and conifers in its native range, including a Chinese variant of Japanese Red Cedar (p.73), where mammals and birds disperse its seeds.

Threats Generally disease-free. Stem rot and leaf blight can occur in nurseries.

The unique leaf shape.

Bark of a mature tree.

Maidenhair-tree – Gymnosperms

91

Angiosperms (broadleaves)

Angiosperm trees are flowering trees whose seeds are enclosed within a fruit (a swollen ovary). They are distinguished from gymnosperms by their flowers, fruits, and the broad form of their leaves.

Their fruits can take many forms, including achene (small, dry fruit often mistaken for a seed), capsule (splits open to reveal seed), drupe (fleshy fruit containing one or more hard, stony seeds), nut (single-seeded fruit enclosed in a hard shell), pome (large, fleshy portion of tissue with shrivelled remains of sepals and stamens opposite the stem) and samara (winged seed).

Most broadleaves are deciduous, but a few are evergreen. They produce hardwood timber, which has a more complex structure than the softwood timber produced by conifers (see p.37).

Angiosperm trees are a diverse group, split into more than 20 families (species included in this book are in parentheses):

- Salicaceae (willows, poplars)
- Juglandaceae (walnuts)
- Betulaceae (birches, alders, Hazel, Hornbeam)
- Fagaceae (European Beech, Sweet Chestnut, oaks)
- Ulmaceae (elms)
- Moraceae (mulberries)
- Magnoliaceae (Tulip-tree)
- Platanaceae (planes)
- Rosaceae (hawthorns, whitebeams, service-trees, Rowan, pears, cherries)
- Fabaceae (Black Locust, Common Gorse)
- Buxaceae (Box)
- Aquifoliaceae (Holly)
- Aceraceae (maples, Sycamore)
- Hippocastanaceae (Horse Chestnut)
- Rhamnaceae (Alder and Purging Buckthorns)
- Tiliaceae (limes)
- Elaeagnaceae (Sea Buckthorn)
- Cornaceae (Dogwood)
- Ericaceae (Strawberry-tree)
- Oleaceae (Common Ash)
- Bignoniaceae (Indian Bean)
- Adoxaceae (Elder, Guelder-rose, Wayfaring-tree)
- Celastraceae (Spindle)

Angiosperm identification

Leaves and buds are the most reliable form of identification for broadleaves. This simple key should help you narrow down the identity of a tree by its buds or leaves.

Definitions:

- **foliage:** deciduous or evergreen
- **buds:** alternate or opposite along shoot (also applies to leaves)
- **leaves:** single or compound (when each leaf is made up of many leaflets)
- **shape:** descriptions of leaf shape
- **margins:** descriptions of the border of the leaf
- **veins:** radiated from a central point at base of leaf, or branched from midrib

Deciduous foliage

Buds	Leaves	Shape	Margins	Veins	See	Page
alternate	single	fan	scalloped	radiated	Maidenhair-tree	93
		heart	serrate	branched	Black Mulberry	153
					Italian Alder	127
					Large-leaved Lime	213
					Small-leaved Lime	211
		lanceolate	entire	branched	Sea Buckthorn	215
			serrate	branched	Common Osier	115
					Crack Willow	113
					Grey Willow	111
					White Willow	107
		lobed	entire	branched	Common Hawthorn	163
					Midland Hawthorn	161
					Tulip-tree	155
					Wild Service-tree	171
					Pedunculate Oak	145
					Red Oak	147
					Sessile Oak	143
					Turkey Oak	139
		oval	crenate	branched	Aspen	105
			entire	branched	Alder Buckthorn	209
					European Beech	135
					Goat Willow	109
			serrate	branched	Bird Cherry	183
					Blackthorn	189
					Cherry Plum	185
					Common Pear	177
					Common Whitebeam	165
					Crab Apple	175
					Domestic Apple	173
					Field Elm	151
					Goat Willow	109
					Hazel	133
					Hornbeam	131
					Wild Cherry	181
					Wild Pear	179
					Wild Plum	187
					Wych Elm	149

Evergreen foliage

Buds	Leaves	Shape	Margins	Veins	See	Page
alternate	single	lobed	spined	branched	Holly Holm Oak	*197* *141*
		oval	serrate	branched	Strawberry-tree	*219*
		spine	N/A	N/A	Common Gorse	*191*
opposite	single	oval	entire	branched	Box	*195*

Deciduous foliage (continued)

Buds	Leaves	Shape	Margins	Veins	See	Page
(alternate continued)	(single continued)	(oval continued)	sharp-serrated	branched	Hornbeam Sweet Chestnut	*131* *137*
		palmately lobed	entire	radiated	London Plane Oriental Plane White Poplar	*159* *157* *97*
		racquet	serrate	branched	Black Alder	*129*
		triangular	lobulated	branched	Grey Poplar	*99*
			serrate	branched	Downy Birch Silver Birch Black Poplar Lombardy Poplar	*125* *123* *103* *101*
	compound	palmate	serrate	branched	Horse Chestnut	*205*
		pinnate	entire	branched	Black Locust Common Walnut	*193* *121*
			serrate	branched	Black Walnut Caucasian Wingnut Rowan Service-tree	*119* *117* *167* *169*
opposite	single	heart	entire	branched	Indian Bean	*223*
		lobed	serrate	radiated	Guelder-rose	*229*
		oval	entire	branched	Dogwood	*217*
		oval	serrate	branched	Purging Buckthorn Spindle Wayfaring-tree	*207* *231* *227*
		palmately lobed	entire	radiated	Field Maple Norway Maple Sycamore	*199* *201* *203*
	compound	pinnate	serrate	branched	Common Ash Elder	*221* *225*

White Poplar *Populus alba*

A large tree, often prominent in the landscape thanks to its white shimmering leaves and pale twigs.

Biology Native to central and southern Europe, but thought to be introduced in Britain and Ireland. Wind-pollinated and dioecious (separate male and female trees), with red male catkins and pale green female catkins. Fluffy white seeds are distributed easily by the wind, and are very successful at germinating in damp soils.

Identification Trees nearly always lean, rugged dark bark at base, smoother pale above where lenticels (dark diamond-shaped pores) are arranged horizontally on trunk. Shoots and rounded buds are both pale, covered in dense white woolly hairs. Leaves lobed (similar to maples), with bright white undersides which remain pale and hairy. *Compare with Grey Poplar (p.99): leaves less lobed and rounded, becoming less white through summer, buds more pointed. Compare with Black Poplar (p.103): twigs similar but leaves distinct.*

Culture Not often planted but a common tree that is completely naturalised. Can be easily grown by taking cuttings. Often found along field margins and near water. Trees sucker so can produce dense thickets of clones. Tolerant of sea winds, and makes an excellent windbreak.

Biodiversity Catkins a good early source of pollen for insects. Larvae of many moth species feed on leaves. Often host to Mistletoe.

Threats Generally robust, but can be damaged by various fungi, rusts, canker and poplar scab.

Bark of mature tree.

Pointed lobed leaves with pale undersides.

Grey Poplar *Populus × canescens*

One of our largest broadleaves, with a massive spreading crown. Can form dense clonal stands, growing from suckers.

Biology Grey Poplar is a naturally occurring hybrid between White Poplar and Aspen, hence the '×' in its scientific name. Dioecious with most trees being male, producing purple catkins. Females partially fertile. Propagates mainly by suckering from adventitious buds along its roots.

Identification Trees usually lean, with large, heavy branches curving downwards at the top of a mature specimen, up to 40m tall. Trunks rugged at base and smooth above. Shoots brown-grey, covered initially in white woolly hairs which disappear during growing season. Leaves rounded-triangular with lobulated margins (pointed lobes), initially white and woolly but later mostly hairless and becoming darker. *Compare with White Poplar (p.97): bark paler, leaves more deeply lobed, and both leaves and shoots remain hairy. Widespread except Scotland.*

Culture A common tree which can be easily grown by taking cuttings. Grows very vigorously, especially in damp and fertile soils. Makes an effective windbreak, and tolerates sea winds. Can drop large branches in strong winds.

Biodiversity Large birds, including raptors, like to nest in its spreading crown. Insects collect pollen and feed on leaves.

Threats Generally robust, but can be damaged by various fungi, rusts, canker and poplar scab.

Rounded-triangular leaves with pointed lobes.

Heavy branching but fast growth.

Lombardy Poplar   *Populus nigra var. italica*

The distinctive slender columnar shape of Lombardy Poplar makes it one of the easiest trees to identify. Named after a region in northern Italy, where it was first discovered.

Biology A naturally occurring variety of Black Poplar (dioecious) and a common cultivar provided by tree nurseries. Trees are always male, producing green-red catkins in spring. Absence of female catkins means no seed fluff is produced.

Identification A tall (30m) fastigiate tree whose branches grow almost vertically, parallel to the trunk, which is often divided. Commonly planted for windbreaks or along roadsides, so seen in linear formation. Buds alternate along branch and pointed. Leaves triangular, margins serrate and crenate. *Compare with hybrids of Lombardy Poplar arising from crosses with other Black Poplars. For example, the cultivar 'Plantierensis',* *produced by crossing with* Populus nigra *subsp.* betulifolia *(p.103), can be male or female, has hairy leaf stalks early in season, trunk often prominently burred.*

Culture Vigorous-growing tree but quite short-lived (*c.*50 years). Thrives in rich and wet soils. Can shed stems and branches, and prone to windblow when mature. Vigorous root system, so trees best planted away from buildings. 'Plantierensis' is better adapted to Britain and Ireland than true Lombardy, often with fuller canopies.

Biodiversity No special associated wildlife.

Threats Cytospora canker (fungal), various bacterial cankers, leaf spots and rusts.

Foliage.

Triangular leaves with toothed margins.

Black Poplar *Populus nigra* subsp. *betulifolia*

A large, majestic native tree species which thrives on floodplains and along riverbanks, famously depicted in John Constable's *The Hay Wain* (1821).

Biology Locally native to England and Wales, but also widely planted, with uncertain status in Ireland. Dioecious, with males producing red catkins and female green catkins producing silky white-haired seeds that are distributed easily in the lightest of winds. Female trees are rare, perhaps just 600 specimens. Fertile seeds are much more likely to be a result of hybridising with other Poplar species.

Identification Impressive broad crown of upwards sweeping branches. Trunk usually leans, bearing branches low down, and commonly very gnarly with burr growth. Leaves quite small (7cm) and triangular in shape with pointed tips, smelling mildly of balsam, serrate margins. Buds pointed. Uncommon in northern Britain and south-west England. *Compare with Black Poplar cultivars: although Lombardy Poplar (p.101) distinct with columnar form.*

Culture Female trees rarely planted due to the 'nuisance' of their copious fluffy seeds. Mostly propagated using cuttings. Makes an elegant specimen tree near watercourses, but not normally found growing in a woodland.

Biodiversity Pollen attracts insects in spring, while foliage favoured by many moths including the Poplar Hawk-moth. Effective stabilising riverbanks, its roots creating habitat for Otter and Kingfisher.

Threats Prejudice against female trees has limited its genetic diversity. Can be infected by bacterial canker, leaf rusts and honey fungus.

Triangular leaves with pointed tips.

Bark of young tree.

Pointed winter buds.

Aspen *Populus tremula*

An elegant tree, which in summer can be identified by sound alone, thanks to its flattened petioles, which allow leaves to tremble in the gentlest of breezes, hence its other common name 'Quaking Aspen'.

Biology A poplar species with a huge native range, spreading across Japan, Russia, North Africa and Europe. Hybridises with White Poplar (p.97) to produce Grey Poplar (p.99). Dioecious, with female trees producing green catkins which when fertilised release fluffy seeds. Trees readily grow suckers, producing large clonal stands of identical trees. Slow-growing and not long-lived but via clones can endure for thousands of years.

Identification Typically up to 25m tall and slender. Cream-coloured bark with diamond-shaped lenticels. Lacks balsam smell of other poplars. Buds are very sharp-pointed, arranged spirally along twig. Leaves round with curved blunt teeth, initially covered in downy hairs but soon smooth, petioles (leaf stalks) flattened near leaf. In autumn, foliage turns bright golden-yellow.

Culture Thrives in sunny places and moist soils, but also grows on rocky outcrops. Easily propagated by taking cuttings.

Biodiversity A pioneer species, and a favourite of the Beaver. Associated with a myriad of insects. Old trees often have hollow stems, popular with nesting birds.

Threats Generally healthy but prone to several fungal diseases, including cankers, leaf rusts and poplar scab.

Bark quite smooth.

Foliage in summer.

Rounded leaves with curved blunt teeth and very thin petiole.

White Willow *Salix alba*

In a family with some 450 species, variously called willows, withies, sallows and osiers, White Willow is perhaps the most majestic and easily identified of all willows.

Biology One of 18 native willow species and *c.*27 hybrids. Dioecious, with flowers (catkins) wind- and insect-pollinated. Tiny seeds enveloped in silky hairs, and easily wind-dispersed.

Identification A large (30m) impressive tree, often leaning, with a canopy distinctly tinted silvery white in summer. Heavily branched, strongly ascending yet with drooping tips. Also commonly pollarded. Flat buds pressed close to shoots, both covered in downy hairs, alternate. Leaves long and narrow, covered with silky white hairs, finely serrate margins. *Compare with Crack Willow (p.113): leaves similarly slender but longer without haired surfaces, instead darker glossy green. Compare with Common Osier (p.115): max. height 10m and bushy, leaves even more slender and crinkled.*

Culture Easily propagated using cuttings. Favours deep and fertile soils, in wet areas. Trees can be pollarded to improve access or safety, or where traditional in the landscape. Its bark and leaves contain salicylic acid, used in manufacture of aspirin.

Biodiversity An important tree species in riparian habitats. Good source of pollen and nectar early in the year. Multitudes of insects feed on leaves. Nesting and roosting sites for birds.

Threats Watermark bacteria, causing leaf wilt and dieback. Also leaf rusts.

Leaves long and narrow, finely serrated margins.

Bark of young tree.

Goat Willow *Salix caprea*

An abundant tree that demands attention in early spring when the distinctive catkins on male trees causes the canopy to come alive with humming insects.

Biology Dioecious. Male trees produce initially grey and furry, then golden-yellow catkins; females more demure but larger green catkins appear a little later, soon releasing small fluffy seeds carried in the wind.

Identification Among all willows, most likely to be seen away from rivers and watercourses. Medium height (20m) and domed canopy. Bark criss-crossed with diamond-shaped ridges. Male catkins appear in early spring before leaves. Shoots dull grey to red, more stocky than most other willows, bearing rounded yellow-brown buds, alternate protruding outwards from shoots. Leaves oval, felty texture on underside, undulating serrate margins and distinctive twisted leaf tip. *Compare with Grey Willow (p.111).*

Culture Rarely planted, but very adept at spreading naturally. Grows in all but the driest sites, and sandy or chalky soils. Likes full sun. Can be easily propagated by taking cuttings. Twigs quite brittle, so not used for weaving, but make an excellent drawing charcoal.

Biodiversity Loved by bumblebees and hoverflies in spring. Leaves are the main food plant for the caterpillars of the Purple Emperor butterfly (which feed at night), and larvae of many moths such as Sallow Kitten and Lunar Hornet Clearwing.

Threats A fungus can cause Goat Willow cankers to grow on branches, causing dieback.

Male catkins in early spring.

Bark criss-crossed.

Oval leaves are felt-like.

Tree covered in male catkins in spring.

Grey Willow *Salix cinerea*

Also known as Grey Sallow, this small native willow is very abundant, found throughout Britain and Ireland. It is sometimes grouped with its close relative the Goat Willow, together collectively known as common sallows.

Biology Dioecious. Male trees produce golden-yellow catkins, females greener catkins that appear a few weeks later. Releases small fluffy seeds which are dispersed by the wind.

Identification A small willow, reaching a maximum height of 15m. Bark dark grey with shallow ridges. Shoots are slightly hairy, as are reddish, alternate buds which are held close to shoots. Distinctive stipules (outgrowths at the base of petioles) are an important identifying feature. Elliptical leaves become wider in outer half, finely serrate. *Compare with Goat Willow (p.109):*

more likely on drier sites, larger catkins on male trees, leaves oval with twisted tip, without stipules, buds point outwards.

Culture Easily propagated by taking cuttings, while wind-dispersed seeds result in widespread natural regeneration.

Biodiversity Bees and hoverflies attracted to male catkins in early spring. Leaves are a food plant for the Purple Emperor butterfly's caterpillars, and larvae of many moth species, in turn attracting feeding birds.

Threats Watermark disease, anthracnose, scab and rusts.

Bark has shallow ridges.

Male catkins in spring.

Elliptical leaves become wider towards tips.

Crack Willow *Salix fragilis*

The Crack Willow's slender stems are favoured by basket makers and weavers, but side shoots break away easily and noisily.

Biology Most botanists believe it is an archaeophyte (ancient introduction). Dioecious, modest yellow-green catkins of both sexes appearing in spring. Insect-pollinated but seeds often sterile. Snapped twigs can be carried by water to lodge in soft mud, where they readily propagate. Readily hybridises with other willows, especially White Willow.

Identification A medium-sized tree to 25m, often with short trunk and wide-spreading branches, which remain erect. Often pollarded. Leaves lance-shaped (slender and long to 15cm) and hairless, glossy green with blue-green underside, margins finely serrate. Twigs snap easily at junctions with branches with a distinctive crack. *Compare with White Willow (p.107): mature trees taller, branch tips weep, twigs less easy to snap, leaves covered in silky hairs. If tree is similar to Crack Willow but taller, could be a hybrid with White Willow.*

Culture Easily propagated by taking cuttings. Loves to grow by rivers, canals and lakes. Historically pollarded to yield willow rods for weaving, and foliage to feed livestock.

Biodiversity Good early source of pollen for insects. Many birds roost and nest in larger trees. Old pollarded trees can host secondary tree species, especially hawthorn, whose roots feed on the rotting willow trunk.

Threats Watermark disease, anthracnose, scab and rusts.

Bark.

Lance-shaped leaves and catkins in spring.

Common Osier *Salix viminalis*

Sometimes known as the Basket Willow, Common Osier provides superior material for weaving.

Biology Considered an archaeophyte (ancient introduction), except in southern England where native. Widely cultivated, propagated by taking cuttings. Many cultivars, some with different coloured stems, produced for basket-making.

Identification Grows to 10m in height with an erect, bushy structure. Trunk short with scaly bark. Yellow-brown dull shoots grow straight and vigorously, initially hairy but soon smooth. Buds green, held tight to shoots, clustering closely together. Leaves are very slender (20cm x 1cm), and distinctly crinkled, dark green above and pale underside. Leaf margins finely serrate. *Compare with White Willow (p.107): mature trees much larger, leaves less slender and not crinkled.*

Culture Fast-growing, thriving in wet soils. Tolerates sea winds, and effective at absorbing heavy metals, so often planted on contaminated ex-industrial sites. Dense root mats help stabilise riverbanks. Plant closely together (creating 'withy stands') and cut regularly to yield stems of suitable diameter for weaving. Can also provide light screening or hedge, or living sculptures.

Biodiversity Early source of pollen. Foliage attracts larvae of many insects, in turn feeding birds, who also find shelter in dense canopies.

Threats Watermark disease which causes dieback. Also, scab and rusts.

Rough scaly bark.

Slender leaves are paler underneath.

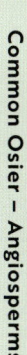

Caucasian Wingnut *Pterocarya fraxinifolia*

Originating in the Caucasus, this large broadleaved tree may prove well adapted to a changing climate in Britain and Ireland.

Biology Introduced in 1782, native to northern Iran, Turkey and Ukraine where it grows in moist soils on floodplains and along riverbanks. Monoecious, and a member of the walnut family. Prominent male catkins in summer. Fruits are green nuts with angled wings (1cm) which help dispersal by wind, but often waterborne. Trees also regenerate with suckers, creating dense thickets.

Identification Can reach 35m tall, often with a short trunk before branching heavily. Dark bark deeply fissured with criss-crossed ridges. Thick shoots, which when cut open at an angle reveal a chambered pith (like walnuts, but not hickories), bearing naked buds. Leaves compound, up to 60cm long, with 9–21 leaflets whose bases have no discernible stalk, overlapping the rachis (midrib), smell of lemon when crushed. *Compare with Black Walnut (p.119) or walnut hybrids: buds protected by scales, shorter leaves (max. 40cm), usually fewer leaflets borne on short petioles (stalks) away from rachis, fruit is a large nut in drupe without wings.*

Culture Makes a good specimen for parks or large gardens. Tolerates seasonal waterlogging and flooding. Due to suckering, provide space to mow around specimen trees. Generally hardy but can be damaged by late spring frosts.

Biodiversity No associated species.

Threats Generally problem-free.

Pendulous male catkin.

Compound leaves, each with up to 21 leaflets.

Canopy showing leaves and catkins.

Black Walnut *Juglans nigra*

A majestic tree introduced in 1656 from North America, where it grows extensively in mixed deciduous forests.

Biology In its native range of the central and eastern US it grows alongside American Ash, Black Cherry, hickories, and Tulip-tree (p.155). Monoecious and wind-pollinated, male flowers are green catkins, females small and barrel-like with feathered stigma. Fruit is a drupe, with a green husk surrounding a nut, dispersed by birds and mammals.

Identification Strong-growing tree up to 35m tall, broadly domed. Shoots brown and downy, with scaled velvety buds. Compound leaves up to 60cm long, 10–23 leaflets but often without a terminal leaflet, finely serrated margins, downy underside. *Compare with Common Walnut (p.131): leaves shorter with 7–11 leaflets, generally more pungent when crushed, however, also hybridises, making identification less obvious. Compare with Caucasian Wingnut (p.117): leaflets overlap rachis, naked buds.*

Culture A light-demanding species which thrives best in the company of other (non-competitive) trees on rich and fertile soils. Avoid waterlogged sites and low areas prone to late frosts. Prune branches only in summer to avoid excessive 'bleeding'. Timber and burrs highly valuable. Husks difficult to remove from nuts.

Biodiversity No special associations.

Threats Can be infected by anthracnose disease and *Phytophthora* root rot. Recently, thousand cankers disease, fatal to all walnut species, has spread from North America to Europe.

Winter shoot.

Drupes.

Bark is quite rough, grey-brown.

Compound leaves, each with 12–23 leaflets.

Common Walnut *Juglans regia*

Introduced by the Romans, this tree is highly prized for its valuable timber and edible nuts, while its leaves provide a natural insect repellent.

Biology Native across Central Asia and the Caucasus, introduced to Europe via the Silk Road, and an archaeophyte in Britain and Ireland. Monoecious and wind-pollinated, male flowers are green catkins, females small and barrel-like with feathered stigma. Fruit a drupe, with a green husk surrounding a nut, dispersed by birds and mammals.

Identification Strongly growing branches, arising from a short trunk, often leaning. Bark smooth and silvery when young, rough and dark when mature. Compound leaves up to 20cm which smell strongly (of juglone) when crushed, 7–11 leaflets, the terminal one usually largest. Drupe husks split in autumn, staining fingers when handling.

Compare with Black Walnut (p.119): more erect tree, longer leaves with 10–23 leaflets, smaller or missing terminal leaflet. Twigs cut diagonally reveal chambered pith, like Black Walnut and Caucasian Wingnut (p.117), but not Common Ash (p.221).

Culture Thrives best in deep, fertile soils, avoiding hollows as frost-sensitive. Needs lots of space but dislikes exposure, growing best with carefully selected companion trees. For nut production, grow in an orchard using a cultivar (e.g. 'Broadview' or 'Lara'), to produce heavy crops in just five years. Prune only in summer to avoid 'bleeding'.

Biodiversity No special associations.

Threats Thousand cankers disease.

Flushing bud in spring.

Compound leaf with 7–11 leaflets.

Male catkins.

Drupes.

Silver Birch *Betula pendula*

Silver Birch adds a flash of brilliance to a woodland throughout the year, while its light and dainty foliage enhances any garden.

Biology One of three birch species native to Britain alongside Downy Birch and Dwarf Birch (*Betula nana*); the latter is a scarce upland species and non-native to Ireland. Silver Birch is a real pioneer, often the first tree to grow on abandoned industrial sites and ungrazed land. Monoecious with pendulous catkins, producing small two-winged seeds distributed by the wind.

Identification An elegant airy tree (to 25m) with pendulous branch tips. Trunk silver-white, often papery, becoming often dark and ruggedly corky at base. Shoots red-brown with tiny white spots, and hairless. Leaves triangular with double-toothed serrate margins, and hairless underneath. *Compare with Downy Birch (p.125): branches do not weep, shoots and leaves covered in fine, downy hairs, leaf shape more teardrop shaped with toothed margins more uniform. However, hybridisation readily occurs, making identification problematic.*

Culture Easy to establish by planting, providing important role as a 'nurse' for other tree species, casting a light shade. Quite light-demanding and generally not long-lived. High-prune stems to produce quality timber.

Biodiversity Supports hundreds of insect species, while seeds loved by small birds like Siskins and Redpolls. Woodpeckers nest in hollow trunks. Associated with wide diversity of fungi, especially fly agaric.

Threats Generally robust and healthy. Fungal pathogens can cause dieback, and prone to honey fungus.

Beautiful papery bark.

Triangular leaves with double-toothed serrate margins.

Downy Birch *Betula pubescens*

Often overlooked and mistaken for Silver Birch, its dainty relative, Downy Birch is an important species in many habitats, especially in our uplands.

Biology More widespread in Ireland than Silver Birch, found throughout both countries, with strongholds in western regions. A pioneer species, providing 'nurseries' for other tree species, like Scots Pine (p.63) in Caledonian pinewoods. Monoecious with pendulous catkins, producing small two-winged seeds distributed by the wind.

Identification A light-branching tree (to 25m). Trunk red-brown, becoming silver with age. Branches thin and do not weep. Shoots red-brown, covered with fine, downy hairs. Leaves teardrop-shaped with serrate single-toothed margins, while petioles and undersides both finely hairy. *Compare with Silver Birch (p.123): trunk more silvery when young, papery bark, branches weep, shoots and leaves not hairy, leaf shape more obviously triangular with double-toothed margins.*

Culture Hardy and tolerant of extreme cold, and can grow in wet soils and exposed locations. Easy to establish by planting, or by simply preventing browsing by mammals where it can form pure stands. An ecosystem pioneer, helping other larger and longer-living trees to establish.

Biodiversity Particularly important species helping nature to recover, for instance in colonising upland areas. Foliage supports hundreds of insects, seeds feed birds, and old trunks provide nesting sites.

Threats Generally robust and healthy. Very prone to honey fungus.

This mature tree is host to lichens and mosses.

Leaves and male catkin.

Leaves have tear-drop shape and serrate single-toothed margins.

Downy Birch – Angiosperms

125

Italian Alder *Alnus cordata*

Native to southern Italy and Corsica, introduced in 1820, this is a species which could thrive in Britain under a changing climate.

Biology Monoecious, each tree producing dangling male catkins (10cm), while female catkins (3cm) are a woody cone-like structure. Cones and seeds distributed by wind and water.

Identification Quite narrow columnar crown, up to 28m, and fast-growing. Grey-brown bark quite smooth, splitting vertically. Leaves slightly heart-shaped, glossy (12cm) and smooth, but notice tiny orange hairs underneath where veins join midrib. Leaf stalks long and thin, meaning trees rustle loudly in a breeze. *Compare with Black Alder (p.129): more likely found in wet ground, leathery leaves with blunt tips, smaller female 'cones.'*

Culture A pioneer tree, capable of growing in poor and damaged soils (including sites too dry for Black Alder). Has a symbiotic relationship with a bacterium, which forms nodules on its roots, converting nitrogen absorbed from the atmosphere by its leaves to ammonia, which is released to the soil, improving fertility and growing conditions for neighbouring trees. A good companion tree in new plantations alongside high-value broadleaves, although its own timber is most suitable for biomass. Highly suitable for shelterbelts and agroforestry.

Biodiversity No special associations with wildlife, but an important ecosystem engineer.

Threats Some susceptibility to *Phytophthora alni*.

Grey-brown bark is quite smooth.

Glossy leaves and female catkins.

Live male catkins (left) hang next to old woody female catkins.

Black Alder *Alnus glutinosa*

Black (or Common) Alder is a familiar sight on riverbanks as it is a specialist wetland species, happiest with its roots in water. Charcoal made from its wood was once important in gunpowder manufacture.

Biology Monoecious, each tree producing dangling male catkins (6cm), while oval female green catkins (2cm) become woody and cone-like in structure. 'Cones' and seeds distributed by water, as both float.

Identification Quite distinctive medium-sized tree (to 28m) growing in wet places, with twisting branches clad in red male catkins in winter and woody 'cones' through much of the year. Mauve-tinged buds on short stalks, alternate. Leaves are blunt-tipped sometimes indented ('racquet-shaped'), leathery surfaced, wavy serrate margins. *Compare with Italian Alder (p.127): glossy leaves with pointed tips, female 'cones' larger. Compare with Alder Buckthorn (p.209): leaves similar with rounded tips but less thick and leathery, otherwise many differences.*

Culture Prefers moist or wet soils, but otherwise very hardy. Establishes and grows rapidly. Nitrogen-fixing capabilities (as with Italian Alder) help improve soil condition. A good nurse with other tree species. Can be coppiced, and generally tolerant of browsing. Not a long-lived tree (60–100 years).

Biodiversity Roots protect riverbanks, and provide spawning sites for fish. Leaves consumed by many insects, including aquatic species.

Threats Distributed in water and soil, *Phytophthora alni* is a significant pathogen causing dieback or death.

Rounded leaves are blunt-tipped.

Alder tongue gall growths emerge from immature female catkins.

Male catkins dangle next to female woody catkins.

Hornbeam *Carpinus betulus*

Producing one of our hardest timbers, its name may mean it is hard as horn, or may refer to a yoke (a beam between horns).

Biology Monoecious, producing prominent yellow catkins in spring, and diminutive yellow-green flowers. Fruit a samara, the seed enclosed in a three-lobed papery bract, hanging in tiers and persisting on the tree throughout winter. Wind distributed.

Identification A large (30m) tree with upright branching. Trunk becoming deeply fluted with age. Bark smooth and grey with vertical cracks. Shoots slender with long buds (8mm), alternate, tips curve inwards. Leaves have double-serrate margins, veins run parallel and deeply impressed, giving a corrugated appearance. Leaves bright yellow in autumn, turning brown and persisting on tree through winter months. *Compare with European Beech (p.135): bark without vertical cracks, buds point away from shoots and straight-pointed, leaves smooth surface and margins.*

Culture Tolerant of shade (but less so than European Beech) and grows better than almost any tree species on cold, heavy and clay soils. Often planted alongside other broadleaves, including oaks, Small-leaved Lime (p.211) and Wych Elm (p.149). Traditionally pollarded or coppiced, producing superior firewood and timber for butchers' blocks, among many uses. Dead leaves retained on branches means it is popular as a hedge plant.

Biodiversity Provides all-year-round shelter for wildlife.

Threats Bark stripping by Grey Squirrel. Can be infected by *Phytophthora* species.

Leaves have serrated margins.

Trunk fluted.

Bark of young tree.

Samara.

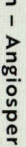

Hazel *Corylus avellana*

Hazel is one of the most important tree species in human history, providing essential materials and fuel. Many of our woodlands were managed to support this productive species, which has high conservation value.

Biology A small (15m tall) monoecious species with a tendency to grow multiple stems. Long, pendulous male catkins release pollen in early spring, dispersed by the wind to fertilise tiny female flowers with red stigma. Seeds (hazelnut) are produced in autumn, distributed by birds and small mammals.

Identification Multi-stemmed stems, bark rough when old but shiny brown when young. Shoots hairy with green buds, alternate. Leaves quite round, rough and hairy, with raggedly serrate margin and an abrupt pointed tip. Nuts partially enclosed in green bracts (involucre) which turn brown when mature. *Compare with Wych Elm (p.149): leaves a little similar, but unique asymmetrical leaf base.*

Culture Hazel grows in all but the most waterlogged soils. Plants are commonly coppiced in woodlands, on regular cycles of six to nine years. Start coppicing three years after planting to create new coppices. Also useful included in hedgerows, particularly for wildlife.

Biodiversity An important food plant for many species, including insects, birds and mammals, such as the endangered Hazel Dormouse. Many fungi are also associated, such as Hazel Gloves. On some western coasts of Ireland and Scotland, pure Hazel woods grow in a rare form of temperate rainforest.

Threats Generally free from pests and diseases.

Maturing hazelnuts.

Pointed leaves with serrate margins.

Male catkins.

European Beech *Fagus sylvatica*

A majestic broadleaved species, whose impressive domed canopy makes it a favourite in designed landscapes, from parks to hilltop clumps.

Biology Considered native only to south-east England and Wales, European Beech was one of the last tree species to colonise when the last ice sheet retreated. Monoecious, with male (tassel-like) and female wind-pollinated flowers (in cups) appearing on the same tree in mid-spring. Seeds (beechmast) distributed by birds and mammals.

Identification One of our tallest broadleaves (up to 40m), with long, sinuous limbs. Bark silver-grey and smooth, never corky. Shoots slender, zigzagging between sharply pointed brown buds. Leaves bright green at first, becoming glossy dark green with hairy margins. Dead leaves on lower branches retained over winter. Beechmast protected by prickly husks on short stalks (2cm). *Compare with Hornbeam (p.131): trunk convoluted,*

dangling female catkins, leaves with toothed margins.

Culture Grows best on neutral or alkaline soils. Does not tolerate drought, nor waterlogging. Shade-tolerant, so often found growing naturally under mature broadleaves of other species, waiting to form the next canopy. A useful species in mixed plantations. Traditionally pollarded in parks and wood pastures.

Biodiversity Pure stands can prevent ground flora growing. However, it is especially valuable towards the end of its relatively short lifespan (*c.*200 years), when its dying wood provides habitat for invertebrates, fungi and lichen.

Threats Considered vulnerable to a warming climate, especially in some strongholds such as the Chiltern Hills. Grey Squirrels can cause serious damage by stripping its thin bark.

Young leaves with hairy margins.

Smooth, silver-grey bark.

Dead leaves retained over winter.

Sweet Chestnut *Castanea sativa*

Native to the Mediterranean, but spread by the Romans, who appreciated its strong, durable timber, which is easily cleft, and its delicious nuts.

Biology Monoecious, producing quite erect hermaphrodite catkins which are female at the base and male towards the tips, and separately clusters of female flowers on shoot tips. Pollen is sticky and sweet smelling, both wind- and insect-dispersed. Up to three nuts (achenes) produced in prickly shells (cupules), distributed by birds and mammals. Rarely fertile further north.

Identification A large (30–35m) tree, which in woodlands can have a noticeably narrow crown compared to other species, but in parklands will be much shorter with a strong, wide crown. Distinctive spiralling bark on older trees. Shoots grey-brown, buds knobbly and hairless. Leaves long and slender, with distinctive sharply serrated margins. Cupules covered with sharp spines.

Culture Grows in most well-drained soils but dislikes shade. Can be coppiced (usually 12–16-year cycles). If grown for timber, usually felled before too large, as timber can develop internal splits (shake). Summers are generally too cool for good nut production in Britain and Ireland, except southern England. Several cultivars available for nut production.

Biodiversity Flowers are an important source of nectar, while nuts are favoured by birds and mammals.

Threats Chestnut blight is a serious concern in Europe.

Leaves in autumn. Note sharp serrated margins.

Cupule with spines open to reveal nuts.

Sweet Chestnut coppice products.

Foliage and fruits in late summer.

Turkey Oak   *Quercus cerris*

Native to the Mediterranean region, this impressive-looking oak species was introduced in 1735 but has since proved unpopular.

Biology Monoecious and wind-pollinated. Seeds (acorns) distributed by birds and mammals.

Identification A fast-growing oak, up to 40m. Branches have a distinctive swelling at junctions. Shoots hairy, buds surrounded by twisted whiskers. Leaves thick, deeply lobed with quite sharp tips, grey felt-like undersides. Acorns (seeds) grow stalkless on shoots, in cups which are roughly whiskered. *Compare with Pedunculate Oak (p.145) and Sessile Oak (p.143): both species without whiskers on buds and acorn cups, leaves less deeply lobed with more rounded tips.*

Culture A robust species capable of growing on heavy clay soils, often planted as an ornamental specimen tree in parks and gardens. Grows rapidly to form an impressive canopy, but has low-value brittle timber. It hosts the Knopper Gall Wasp (*Andricus quercuscalicis*), which spends one generation feeding on its catkins before the subsequent generation infects any neighbouring native oak species, causing alien-like growths to appear on their acorns, often limiting their ability to regenerate naturally. As such, the species is not looked upon favourably by many foresters.

Biodiversity No special associated species.

Threats None.

Bark is similar to other oaks.

Leaves deep-lobed, sharp tips.

Immature acorn cups.

Holm Oak   *Quercus ilex*

One of few broadleaves that is evergreen, this impressive tree stands out in country estates and parks, especially during the winter months.

Biology An evergreen broadleaved tree, introduced from the mixed forests of the Mediterranean in the sixteenth century. Monoecious, producing sprays of male flowers in early summer, coinciding with the drop of the previous season's leaves. Seed is an acorn.

Identification A broad spreading evergreen tree. Bark distinctly dark with small square plates. Its glossy leaves are slightly spiny-lobed (especially on young shoots) and reminiscent of Holly (hence its species name 'ilex'), becoming less spiny on older branches, dark green above with pale green felt-like downy undersides. Acorn dumpy (max. 20mm), roughly equal in size to its felted cup. *Compare with Holly (p.197): leaves glossy on both surfaces.*

Culture Tolerant of pollution and salt-laden winds, even sea spray. Can be clipped into hedges and topiary, but left alone grows a large spreading canopy. Often planted as a specimen tree or to create impressive avenues on estates of stately homes. Severely cold winters can lead to leaf drop. Timber is low value.

Biodiversity Its evergreen canopy provides shelter to wildlife all year round, while its catkins provide a source of nectar for insects in spring, and birds and mammals consume its acorns.

Threats Generally healthy. May thrive in warmer, drier summers in Britain and Ireland projected under a changing climate.

Acorns. Note the smoother margins of older leaves.

Evergreen, glossy leaves, with spiny lobes.

Sessile Oak   *Quercus petraea*

One of our two native oak species, more often found growing naturally in the uplands of northern and western Britain, and in Ireland, where it is also known as Irish or Durmast Oak.

Biology Monoecious, with drooping male catkins and diminutive red female flowers. A pioneer species thanks to its palatable acorns, which are distributed by birds and mammals. Grows a second flush of leaves in summer, called Lammas growth. Heavy seed years (known as mast crops) occur every three to four years.

Identification A stately broadleaved tree (to 40m tall) in fertile sheltered sites, but also grows at high elevations in upland regions, where it can have a twisted and stunted form. Leaves are shallow-lobed on long petioles (stalks), and wedge-shaped at base. Female flowers and later acorns are sessile, meaning without a stem, growing directly on shoots. *Compare with Pedunculate Oak (p.145): more likely to be found growing in lowland areas, especially on heavier soils, leaf petioles shorter, leaves have small backwards-pointing auricles, acorns grow on a peduncle (stalk). Note that Sessile Oak and Pedunculate Oak commonly hybridise, blending their features, making identification problematic.*

Culture Many foresters believe Sessile Oak is the better choice between our two native oaks as a productive forest species.

Biodiversity Alongside the Pedunculate Oak, supports the richest diversity of wildlife species of any tree.

Threats Detailed under Pedunculate Oak.

Leaves wedge-shaped at base with long petiole.

Acorn has no petiole.

Bark with young leaves.

Pedunculate Oak *Quercus robur*

Often considered the king of trees, this is one of two native oak species, valued as much for its grandeur in the landscape as it is for the utility of its superior timber, and its importance for wildlife.

Biology Monoecious, with drooping male catkins and diminutive red female flowers. A pioneer species thanks to its palatable acorns, which are distributed by birds and mammals. Grows a second flush of leaves in summer, called Lammas growth. Heavy seed years (known as mast crops) occur every three to four years.

Identification A majestic, long-lived (more than 1,000 years) tree growing to 38m tall in woodlands, but with a huge spreading canopy when open-grown in fields, hedges and parkland. Leaves are quite deeply lobed, on short petioles, leaf base has tiny lobes (auricles) curving backwards. Acorns grow on a stalk (peduncle). *Compare with Sessile Oak (p.143).*

Culture Both native oaks are often grown in mixture with other species to help promote their growth. Sudden exposure to sunlight can cause trees to produce proliferation of tiny epicormic shoots. Traditionally, oaks are grown as a 'standard' over coppiced trees, especially Hazel (p.133).

Biodiversity Supports more than 2,000 other species (including 326 obligate). Notable associated species include Purple Hairstreak butterfly. Seeds distributed by mammals and birds, especially Jays.

Threats Acute oak decline affects trees in southern Britain. A recent pest is the Oak Processionary moth (see p.33), also harmful to humans.

Rough furrowed bark.

Lobed leaves with auricle at base on short petiole.

Male catkins.

Acorn with growth from knopper gall.

Red Oak *Quercus rubra*

Native to North America and introduced in 1724, its large leaves can be very colourful in the autumn.

Biology Monoecious wind-pollinated tree with hanging male catkins and small female red flowers growing between shoot and leaf stalks. Seed is an acorn which takes two years to mature.

Identification Similar appearance to native oaks, but branches noticeably straighter and bark relatively smooth. Shoots grey and hairless except when young. Leaves emerge quite late in spring, large (up to 20cm) and sharply lobed with multiple whiskered teeth per lobe. Acorns smaller than those of native oaks, and when mature the seed is much larger than the cup.

Culture Seed is rarely viable except in southern areas. Often planted in parks and gardens for its autumn colours, but often a little disappointing compared to the display in its native range, due to the cooler climate in Britain and Ireland. Grows exceptionally well on heavy clay soils. Quite shade-tolerant and coppices well. Timber quite valuable but prone to forking, requiring high pruning, although less prone to epicormic shoots than native oaks.

Biodiversity No specific species, although insects feed on its pollen in spring.

Threats Foliage is palatable to deer, while thin bark is readily damaged by Grey Squirrels. With a warming climate, may become invasive.

Leaves in autumn.

Maturing acorns.

Bark is smooth compared to other oaks.

Wych Elm *Ulmus glabra*

The only species of elm native to both Britain and Ireland among some six species thought to be endemic in Europe. Most likely to be found in forests or hedgerows.

Biology A monoecious tree, growing to 25m (rarely 30m) tall. Unlike all other elm species found in Britain and Ireland, it produces viable seed. It can hybridise with other elm species. Hermaphrodite flowers produced in clusters, wind-pollinated. Fruit are small samaras (winged seeds) dispersed by wind.

Identification Broad crown becoming domed. Bark smooth grey when young, becoming darker with long corky ridges. Shoots quite dark and stiffly haired, as are its purple-black buds. Red-green flowers appear before leaves in spring. Ovoid leaves up to 18cm (largest of any native tree) becoming wider towards tip, which is abruptly pointed, stiff hairs on upper surface, doubly serrated (toothed) margins, distinctly asymmetrical leaf bases, almost without any petiole (stalk) on one side. Samara wing tips notched. *Compare with Field Elm (p.151): although hybrids common; if suckering present, more likely to be a hybrid.*

Culture Propagate by seed, not cuttings, to promote genetic diversity. Prefers some sun, thriving in hedgerows and woodland edges.

Biodiversity Food plant of the White-letter Hairstreak butterfly. Seeds enjoyed by finches.

Threats With its ability to reproduce via seed, Wych Elm is genetically diverse and more resistant to Dutch elm disease than other elm species, though not immune.

Ovoid leaves, wider towards tip, serrated margins.

Samaras each contain a single seed.

Mature seeds are a vibrant pink.

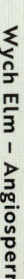

Wych Elm – Angiosperms

149

Field Elm *Ulmus minor* agg.

Field Elm is a term adopted by botanists to describe several closely related species, including English Elm, once an iconic tree in our landscape before Dutch elm disease (DED) arrived in waves during the twentieth century.

Biology The taxonomy of the elms is very complex and still disputed. While *Ulmus minor* refers to Field Elm, 'agg.' means it is an aggregate of closely related elm varieties including Cornish, English, Smooth-leaved and Wheatley. These varieties are native to Britain, but most likely only in southern regions. Propagation is mostly clonally via suckers.

Identification Mature English Elm trees were historically instantly recognisable thanks to their distinctive tall (45m) and narrow form with domed tops. Now usually reduced to small trees (max. height 10m, stem diameter 10cm) and suckering scrub in hedgerows. English Elm develops corky wings along branches, other species less so (*compare with Field Maple p.199*), leaves rough and crinkled, red hairs on shoots and buds.

Culture Grows best in fertile agricultural soils, but often found in roadside hedgerows. Propagated by cuttings. Light-demanding but very tolerant of different conditions. Some Field Elm varieties can be more resistant to DED and grow larger than English Elm.

Biodiversity Once important hosts of wildlife, but now limited due to DED.

Threats DED affects trees once a trunk is about 10cm in thickness, when it becomes attractive to wood-boring elm bark beetles, which innocently spread the fungus. Very few trees are unaffected but large specimens can still occasionally be discovered.

Rough, crinkled leaves.

Corky growth on young branch.

A rare healthy stand of mature Field Elm.

Field Elm – Angiosperms

151

Black Mulberry *Morus nigra*

Originating in western Asia and introduced in the seventeenth century, Black Mulberry is prized for its delicious but delicate fruits which look like giant blackberries.

Biology Trees can be either dioecious or monoecious, sometimes changing sex over time. Wind-pollinated. Male flowers diminutive catkins, female flowers appear in scaly clusters before swelling to produce a large black drupe, technically not a berry but made up of a cluster of multiple separate swollen drupelets. Dispersed by feeding birds and mammals.

Identification Rarely more than 10m tall, but often broad, often severely leaning with strong, twisting branches, in large gardens or country parks. Bark orangey and scaly, shoots with stiff hairs, buds purple. Leaves large (to 12cm) and heart-shaped with serrated margins, glossy appearance but quite rough, especially on underside. *Compare with*

White Mulberry (not featured): rarely cultivated but the favoured plant of the silkworm, leaves glossy and mostly smooth.

Culture Grow from seed or cuttings, or purchase a known variety such as 'Chelsea'. Plant in well-drained soils. Very drought-resistant. Fruiting does not begin until trees are at least eight years old. Picking the delicate fruit stains hands and clothing! Nets may be needed to prevent birds feeding on fruit before picking. Leaning stems and spreading branches can be propped up.

Biodiversity No special associated wildlife.

Threats A warming climate may favour mulberry fruit production.

Immature drupe.

Large leaves with serrated margins.

Black Mulberry – Angiosperms

Tulip-tree *Liriodendron tulipfera*

Known as 'Yellow Poplar' or 'Tulip Poplar' in its native range, this vigorous hardwood with showy flowers was introduced from the mixed hardwood forests of eastern North America in the seventeenth century.

Biology Despite its American common names, it is unrelated to poplars. In its native range it grows alongside Black Walnut (p.119), hickories and maples. Monoecious with 'perfect' flowers, having male and female reproductive structures (stamens and pistils) in the same flower. Insect-pollinated, producing winged seeds (samaras) distributed by the wind.

Identification Very tall (to 40m), narrow-crowned. Bark quite grey, becoming rough with crisscrossed ridges, aromatic (reminiscent of cucumber). Buds flat, duckbill-like, on short stalks. Large, distinctively lobed (usually four) leaves. Flowers orange-green and tulip-like (5cm), emerging in early summer often hidden among foliage. Seedheads brown and cone-like, consisting of tightly clustered and overlapping samaras.

Culture Favours well-drained soils but will tolerate flooding. Easy to propagate from seeds or cuttings and grows rapidly. Handle plants gently as roots easily damaged. Grows well in company with other hardwoods, but dislikes heavy shade. Leaves add autumnal colour. Versatile timber is light and easy to work, and popular with wood carvers.

Biodiversity Insects feed on nectar.

Threats Few serious threats. Likely to thrive under a warming climate and a candidate for future timber production.

Rough, grey bark with crisscrossed ridges.

Leaves and a tulip-like flower.

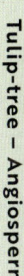

Oriental Plane *Platanus orientalis*

Native to the Himalayas, Caucasus and Mediterranean, this species' large spreading crown has long been appreciated for its cooling shade. Arrived in Britain sometime before 1548.

Biology Naturally grows in riparian areas, but followed spread of ancient civilisations. Much planted for its cooling benefits, especially in southern Europe. Monoecious, and long-lived (500+ years). One of the parent species of the hybrid London Plane. Individual seeds develop in achenes (non-opening hard fruits) each with a hairy tip to aid dispersal by wind, presented together with others in spherical clusters.

Identification Rarely seen outside parks and avenues. Tall (30m) with broad crown. Trunk often short and heavily burred, bark brown plated and flaking. Branches heavy, can weep to ground. Shoots with alternate buds. Leaves lobed and deeply palmate, with 1–2 small teeth on lobe shoulders, smelling fresh and earthy. Seed balls hang 3–6 on strings. *Compare with London Plane (p.159): less broad spreading crown, bark often with paler scales, leaves less deeply lobed with three or more teeth on lobe shoulders and less aromatic, seed balls often 2 (but can have up to 6 on a string).*

Culture Excellent urban species but intolerant of salt (e.g. from de-icing roads). Quite frost-sensitive. Can be vigorous in warm and fertile sites. Foliage is attractively shaped, turning bronze and deep crimson in autumn, and much planted for landscape.

Biodiversity No special wildlife but valuable in urban places.

Threats Canker stain, Massaria and anthracnose diseases among several threats.

Brown, plated and flaking bark.

Leaves lobed and deeply palmate.

Seed balls (achenes).

London Plane *Platanus × hispanica*

A popular street tree, London Plane is tolerant of urban pollution and often brutal pruning regimes, and has been responsible for greening many of our cityscapes since being discovered in the seventeenth century.

Biology A fertile hybrid between Oriental Plane and the American Sycamore (*Platanus occidentalis*: unrelated to Sycamore p.203). Monoecious, producing achenes in spherical seed balls. Several named varieties have been cultivated with specific attributes, including peeling bark or crown architecture.

Identification Tall (40m+), often multi-stemmed with long, strong-growing limbs. Street trees often pollarded and heavily pruned, resulting in heavy limbs with masses of finer shoots. Bark scaly and plated, and variously coloured brown, cream and blue-green. Shoots with alternate buds. Leaves palmate, with three or more small teeth on lobe shoulders. Achenes hang in spherical spiky seed balls, 2–6 per string. *Compare with Oriental Plane (p.157).*

Culture Usually propagated by taking cuttings, particularly to ensure specific varieties. Generally very hardy, not only tolerant of pollution but also extreme cold and drought. Avoid waterlogged soils and heavy shading. Very windfirm but Massaria disease can cause sudden drop of large branches. Seed hairs can cause asthma in humans.

Biodiversity No special wildlife, but provides shelter to urban wildlife.

Threats Canker stain, Massaria and anthracnose diseases among several current threats, while plane wilt is a serious pathogen elsewhere in Europe.

Colourful, plated bark.

Seed balls (achenes).

Palmate leaves with pointed lobes.

Midland Hawthorn *Crataegus laevigata*

Native to Britain but a neophyte in Ireland, Midland Hawthorn is similar to the more frequent and widespread Common Hawthorn yet often overlooked.

Biology Monoecious, with hermaphrodite flowers with 2–3 styles, insect-pollinated, resulting in 2–3 nutlets inside a crimson red pome (fruit) known as a haw.

Identification Infrequent outside stronghold in Midlands, south and east of England. Bushy growth with sharp spines on branches. Small, slightly glossy leaves have three shallow lobes that are mildly cut, never more than halfway to midrib, and almost hairless. White flowers in May, sometimes pink, with 2–3 styles. Crimson fruits contain 2–3 seeds. *Compare with Common Hawthorn (p.163): generally very similar, except leaves deeply cut (more than halfway to midrib) and more obvious hairs on underside, single style in flowers, fruits contain a single seed. Can hybridise with Common Hawthorn.*

Culture Thrives on heavy clay soils. Grown from seed. Can be laid in hedgerows or retained as a small standard tree.

Biodiversity Found in ancient woodland and hedgerows, its thorny canopy provides shelter all year round. Its flowers provide a source of nectar in spring and fruit for birds (e.g. Hawfinch) and mammals in winter.

Threats Generally free of pests and pathogens.

Haws.

Three-lobed leaves, less deeply cut than in Common Hawthorn.

Rough bark.

White flowers with 2–3 styles.

Common Hawthorn · *Crataegus monogyna*

Variously also known as Quickthorn or the May Tree, the white blossom of Common Hawthorn lights up the countryside in late spring, while its thorns prevent livestock from straying.

Biology Monoecious, with hermaphrodite flowers with a single style, insect-pollinated, producing a single nutlet inside a crimson red pome (fruit) known as a haw.

Identification A small tree (up to 10m) yet can live to be hundreds of years old. Bushy growth with sharp spines on branches. Small, slightly glossy leaves with three shallow lobes which are deeply cut, with hair tufts on underside at vein junctions. White, sometimes pink, flowers with a single style, appear in May and are among the last to appear in hedgerows and woodland edges in a sequence which begins with Cherry Plum (p.185), then Blackthorn (p.189). Fruits ripen to crimson, containing a single seed. *Compare with Midland Hawthorn (p.161): but note can also hybridise.*

Culture Grown from seed. Often the main species in hedgerows where it was traditionally favoured to help control livestock, especially when laid to create thicker hedge bases and dense sides. Tolerates frequent and hard cutting.

Biodiversity As the haws hang on trees long into the winter, they are an important source of food during hard times for wildlife. Particularly enjoyed by winter visitors such as Fieldfare, Redwing and Waxwing.

Threats Generally free of pests and pathogens.

White flowers have a single style.

Flowers and leaves. Notice the deeply cut leaves.

Haws in autumn.

Common Whitebeam *Aria edulis*

It may only have a modest stature, but the pale flash of Common Whitebeam's leaves add beauty and diversity to woodland edges and hedgerows, while cultivars are common in parks and gardens.

Biology Monoecious with hermaphrodite (male and female) flowers. Insect-pollinated, producing small red fruit each containing two seeds, distributed mainly by birds.

Identification Less frequent in Ireland and Scotland, most common in central southern England. Rarely more than 15m tall, usually multi-stemmed and stiffly upright. Shoots brown but green when growing in sun, buds alternate, quite large (15mm) and green-scaled, terminal buds hairy. Leaves emerge covered in white downy hairs, soon disappearing from upper surface leaving distinctive pale undersides, margins double-serrate with very subtle lobes. Flowers small and white in flat inflorescence (7cm wide). Fruits crimson red with lenticels, giving a speckled appearance.

Culture With its modest size, flowers and fruit, and attractive summer foliage turning yellow in autumn, it's no wonder this species is popular in small gardens, as are its many cultivars. Also makes an attractive standard in hedgerows. Tolerant of a wide range of soil conditions, light-demanding so usually found along the edges of woodlands.

Biodiversity Its fruits can persist on the tree through the winter but are a favourite of Blackbirds and other thrushes, so rarely remain.

Threats Can be infected by apple canker and fire blight. Mammals, especially deer, like to browse.

Downy undersides of young leaves.

Maturing fruits.

White flowers.

Foliage flashes pale undersides in the wind.

Rowan *Sorbus aucuparia*

Rowan is sometimes known as Mountain Ash, partly because of its hardiness and also its leaves, which are a little similar to those of Common Ash.

Biology Monoecious, producing corymbose heads of hermaphrodite flowers in early summer which are insect-pollinated. Its small pomes (fruits) are distributed mainly by birds.

Identification Grows up to 15m, often with multiple stems which ascend steeply. Bark quite smooth and grey, often with bands of dark lenticels. Buds purple-tinged and haired. Leaves compound pinnate, usually 15 leaflets, with serrated margins, often turning bright yellow-orange in autumn. Flowers creamy white in clusters (May–July). Fruit small (10mm) and scarlet, hanging in clusters. *Compare with Common Ash (p.221): leaflet margins smooth.*

Culture Extremely cold-hardy, and able to withstand many conditions from polluted city gardens to exposed mountainsides. Generate from seed. Tolerates most soils except those waterlogged, but equally intolerant of drought. Prefers sunny sites, either open grown or woodland margins.

Biodiversity Insects feed on its nectar. The plentiful harvest of berries this species provides to birds in winter is significant, especially for both resident and visiting thrushes.

Threats Highly palatable to deer. Projected to lose suitable habitat in Ireland and west Scotland under a changing climate.

Creamy-white clusters of flowers.

Scarlet fruits.

Compound, pinnate leaves with serrated margins.

Service-tree *Cormus domestica*

A rare species, also known as True Service, more common in southern Europe but ancient trees discovered in southern Britain have confirmed its native status.

Biology Monoecious, producing corymbose heads of hermaphrodite flowers in early summer which are insect- and wind-pollinated. Its small pomes (fruits), distributed mainly by birds and mammals, have two forms: *pomifera* (globular and apple-like) or *pyrifera* (pear-like).

Identification Grows up to 20m, with stiff branching habit and broad dome. Bark dark grey, rough and crisscrossed. Shoots grey-brown and shiny, alternate. Buds rounded and bright green. Leaves compound and unevenly pinnate (more leaflets on one side than the other), 15 leaflets with serrated margins, soft hairy undersides. Flowers creamy white in large clusters (May–July). Fruit medium-sized (30mm) and russet-green, turning brown, hanging in clusters. *Compare with Rowan (p.167): similar leaves but not hairy. Compare with Wild Pear (p.179): bark similar but otherwise not easily confused.*

Culture A hardy tree, tolerant of a wide range of soils. Not shade-tolerant. Fruit is edible once bletted or cooked, and once popular for cider-making and medicines (but beware, seeds are poisonous).

Biodiversity Flowers sustain insects, while fruits are a favourite among thrushes, finches and Woodpigeons.

Threats The main threat to this species is its rarity, with small, isolated populations unable to breed and reproduce. Otherwise, could thrive in Britain in a warming climate.

Rough, crisscrossed bark.

Compound, pinnate leaves with serrated margins.

Fruits.

Wild Service-tree *Torminalis glaberrima*

Native only to southern Britain, this uncommon species (also known as the Chequers Tree) is a good indicator of ancient woodland, but has also been widely planted for its autumn colour.

Biology Monoecious, producing corymbose heads of up to 20–30 hermaphrodite flowers in early summer which are insect-pollinated. Its small pomes (fruits) are distributed by small mammals and birds.

Identification Medium-sized (25m), usually single-stemmed and fast-growing. Bark ash grey, becoming scaly with a tendency to peel. Shoots brown and shiny, buds alternate, bright green and rounded. Leaves shiny and sharply lobed, veins branch along the midrib, turning yellow in autumn. Flowers white. Fruit small (15mm), speckled russet-green turning brown. *Compare leaves generally to maples (Field Maple p.199 or Sycamore p.203): buds/leaves opposite along shoots, veins radiate from leaf base.*

Culture Thrives in heavy clay soils. Best grown in forests in the 'sub-canopy', preferring some competition and a little shading. Produces the most valuable timber of any species grown in Europe, and highly prized for veneers. Protect from deer and remove branches to promote timber quality. Fruits once used to make or flavour beers, hence 'Chequers' as a popular name for pubs in England.

Biodiversity Flowers and fruits sustain a wide range of insects, mammals and birds.

Threats Generally healthy. Targeted by browsing deer.

Rough, scaly bark.

Leaves distinctive, with veins branching from midrib.

Maturing pomes (fruits).

Domestic Apple *Malus domestica*

Originating in Central Asia where its ancestor can still be found growing, the Domestic (or Orchard) Apple has been cultivated for its delicious fruit for millennia.

Biology Its ancestor is the wild apple *Malus sieversii*, not Crab Apple. Monoecious with hermaphrodite flowers, but usually not self-fertile (i.e. requires pollen from a neighbouring tree). Insect- and wind-pollinated, fertilised flowers producing a pome (fruit) with seeds at its core. Distributed by birds and mammals. Resulting 'wild' seedlings rarely display the traits of their cultivar parents.

Identification Generally found in parks and gardens, while 'wild escapees' can be found in hedgerows and roadsides, although these are often hybrids. Bark grey-brown. Shoots and buds downy haired. Leaves oblong (10cm) with irregular serrated margins, downy underside. Pink flower buds, opening to pink-white blossoms. *Compare with Crab Apple (p.175).*

Culture Varieties of Domestic Apple are always propagated by taking cuttings, which are grafted onto rootstocks that determine the stature of the tree when mature, from miniature (M27) to large standard (M25). Make sure a pollinating tree is nearby. Trees can be trained into different shapes, including fan and espalier, to cordon, bush or standard. Prune to shape in winter, and when older, remove lateral shoots in summer to improve fruiting. Timber cherished for small items.

Biodiversity Blossom is a favourite for bees and hoverflies. Any fruit left on trees or on the ground below as windfalls are loved by thrushes.

Threats Aphids and Codling Moths are major pests.

Pink-white flowers.

Grey-brown bark.

Fruits in late summer.

Crab Apple *Malus sylvestris*

Our native apple takes its name from the Old English *crabbe*, meaning 'bitter or sharp taste'.

Biology Monoecious with hermaphrodite flowers which are self-compatible. Mostly insect-pollinated, fertilised flowers producing a small pome (fruit) with seeds at its core. Distributed by birds and mammals. Hybridises with Domestic Apple but not thought to have been significant genetically in its domestication.

Identification Distributed across all of Britain (except Scottish Highlands) and Ireland. Broad-domed tree to 10m, with chaotic branching. Bark purple-brown, becoming scaly. Shoots glossy and hairless, buds downy at tips. Leaves glossy (6cm) and mostly hairless, margins softly serrate. Flower buds pink, opening to white blossoms, calyx hairy only on inside surfaces. Fruit small (4cm), yellow, hard, with bitter taste, often persisting on ground after falling. *Compare with*

Domestic Apple (p.173): leaves and buds downy haired, calyx hairy on both surfaces, blossoms pink-tinged, fruit larger.

Culture Thrives in many soils, including heavy clay. Grows best in sunny locations, including woodland edges and hedgerows, although can be included alongside Hazel under well-spaced large trees, such as oaks in a coppice-with-standards system.

Biodiversity Blossom is a favourite for bees and hoverflies. When the fruit falls in autumn, it slowly softens, becoming palatable to mammals and birds, helping sustain wildlife through barren winter months. Often host to Mistletoe.

Threats While it can be infected by various pests and pathogens, the greatest threat is hybridisation with Domestic Apple.

Scaly bark.

Fruits.

Flowers.

Common Pear *Pyrus communis*

The domestic form of Wild Pear, originating in Europe and Asia, is second only to Domestic Apple in its importance as a fruit tree.

Biology Monoecious with hermaphrodite flowers, but usually not self-fertile (i.e. requires pollen from a neighbouring tree). Insect- and wind-pollinated flowers open at same time as foliage. Fertilised flowers produce a pome (fruit) with seeds at its core. Distributed by birds and mammals.

Identification Mostly found growing in gardens and orchards. Trees (15m) are often steeply ascending, and sparse branches. Bark dark brown, becoming rough with age. Shoots glossy with pointed buds. Leaves glossy green, oblong sometimes heart-shaped base, tiny rounded-toothed margins. White flowers often appear in dense clusters, before apple blossom. Fruit pear-shaped, gritty texture. *Compare with Wild Pear (p.179).*

Culture Varieties of Common Pear are always propagated by taking cuttings, which are grafted onto rootstocks that determine the stature of the tree when mature. Make sure a pollinating tree is nearby. Water well after planting. There are hundreds of varieties available, some requiring cooking, others making lovely dessert fruit. Fruit is sometimes used to make perry (equivalent to cider made with apples). Timber is highly valued for wood-turning and musical instruments.

Biodiversity Pollinating insects, especially bees, take advantage of its early spring blossoms.

Threats Pear rust is a serious disease causing bright orange leaf spots. Fire blight can reduce fruiting, or even tree death.

Rough bark.

Flowers white, losing petals when fertilised.

A maturing fruit.

Wild Pear *Pyrus pyraster*

An ancient introduction, probably for its small fruits which are delicious after cooking, while charcoal from its wood has been found dating from the Neolithic period.

Biology Native to Europe and western Asia. Monoecious, hermaphrodite flowers which are insect-pollinated. Flowers open at same time as foliage. Fertilised flowers produce a small pome (fruit) with seeds at its core. Distributed by birds and mammals.

Identification Trees (15m) are often multi-stemmed, with steeply ascending and sparse branches. More likely to be planted than a naturally occurring tree. Distinctly narrow crown and steep branches. Bark grey-brown, with square plates. Shoots are spiny. Leaves oval, small (4cm) and glossy, serrulate margins. Flowers white, appearing in dense clusters before many other flowering trees, except Cherry Plum (p.185). Fruits to 4cm, rounded yellow-green and very hard. *Compare with Common Pear (p.177): shoots not spiny, leaves larger, fruit larger and less round. Compare with Plymouth Pear (not featured): native but very rare, occurring naturally only in Devon and Cornwall, tiny marble-sized fruits.*

Culture Prefers well-drained soils, and very intolerant of shade. Makes an attractive addition to hedgerows and woodland edges. Traditionally used as a rootstock for cultivated varieties of Common Pear. Fine-grained timber is valuable but rarely available.

Biodiversity Attractive to pollinating insects in spring, while fruits are enjoyed by birds and mammals after falling and softening by repeated frosts.

Threats Most threatened by hybridisation with Common Pear as it has a sparse distribution.

Bark grey-brown, small square plates.

Flowers with white petals and red stamen.

Wild Cherry   *Prunus avium*

A magnificent tree (also known as the Gean or Mazzard) with a multitude of qualities, including landscape value, food for wildlife and a highly prized timber.

Biology Large but relatively short-lived (100–150 years). Monoecious, with hermaphrodite flowers, generally not self-fertile. Insect-pollinated, producing small (20mm) drupes (cherry fruit) containing a single seed, ingested and distributed by birds and mammals in their droppings. Also reproduces clonally by suckering.

Identification A tall (30m or more) tree. Distinctive red-brown bark, with dark, craggy horizontal lines of lenticels, sometimes peeling and can produce resin when damaged. Branches grow in whorls. Shoots grey-brown, hairless, buds red-brown and quite large, flower buds clustering. Leaves unfurl bronze-green, becoming large (12cm) and oval, with coarse single-toothed margins. White flowers appear with foliage on single stalks. A mature flowering Wild Cherry is unmistakable along a woodland edge in spring. Cherry fruit green and bitter, ripening to bright dark red and delicious. *Compare with Bird Cherry (p.183).*

Culture Seed source is important to grow quality trees (avoid fruit orchard origin if interested in timber trees). Provide plenty of space and sunlight. Prune only in early summer (when silver leaf disease and bacterial canker are less prevalent) and gradually over years remove lower whorls of branches to promote quality timber. Foliage poisonous to horses.

Biodiversity Valuable for pollinating insects in spring, while fruit sustains birds and mammals in autumn.

Threats Prone to bacterial canker and several other diseases. Foliage palatable to deer.

Red-brown bark – note the horizontal lenticels.

Flowers.

Mature fruits.

Leaves oval with toothed margins.

Bird Cherry *Prunus padus*

The astringent fruits of this tree, known as Hagberry in Scotland, are loved by birds but less so by humans, while its leaves and seeds are poisonous.

Biology Monoecious, with hermaphrodite flowers pollinated by insects, and also self-compatible. Fruit are small (8mm) drupes (fruits) containing a single seed, ingested and distributed by birds and mammals in their droppings.

Identification Less common in Éire and south-west England than elsewhere. Small–medium (15m) tree, branches usually steeply rising and quite fine. Bark grey and finely rough. Shoots grey with white lenticels, alternate sharp buds. Leaves hairless except undersides at vein joints, margins finely and sharp-serrated. Almond-scented white flowers grow on stiff racemes, often upright initially, in late spring. Small black fruits hang in racemes in autumn. *Compare with Wild Cherry (p.181): bark redder with horizontal bands of lenticels and tendency to peel, leaves less sharply toothed, flowers in loose clusters, fruit ripens to red.*

Culture Grows in many different soils, including wet flushes and fens, yet rarely planted, especially in gardens. The bitter fruits are palatable when cooked (and popular in eastern Europe) but the seeds are poisonous when crushed (as are parts of the tree) to humans and dogs.

Biodiversity Flowers attract pollinating insects, while foliage eaten by many caterpillars, including Bird-cherry Ermine moth. Birds, especially finches and thrushes, will pick a tree clean, while mammals enjoy fallen fruits.

Threats Vulnerable to bacterial canker and silver leaf disease.

Bark grey and finely rough.

White flowers on upright racemes.

Leaves have finely serrated margins.

Mature fruits.

Cherry Plum *Prunus cerasifera*

Often confused with Blackthorn, Cherry Plum is usually the first tree to flower in hedgerows and unmissable in spring, before becoming 'invisible' again.

Biology A neophyte known to have been present in Britain since 1597, it is particularly common in England but less so elsewhere in Britain, and in Ireland. It is thought to be one of the parents of Wild Plum. Monoecious, with hermaphrodite flowers, producing small globular fruits. Dispersed by birds and mammals.

Identification Grows up to 15m, with untidy branching habit. Bark dark grey-brown, shoots green when young and hairless, without spines. Leaves bright green, downy along undersides of veins, serrate margins. Flowers pure white, appearing March in south of country, quite pungent. Small (4cm) fruits, variously red to gold, sweet and delicious with large central seed. *Compare with*
Blackthorn (p.189): spined branches and shoots, flowers more creamy coloured, appearing later in season, fruit black and astringent. Compare with Wild Plum (p.187): buds shorter, fruit purple.

Culture Very widely naturalised but probably rarely planted. Thrives in hedges and deserves to be promoted in the landscape for its cheery spring blossom alone. Trees do not sucker much. Can be trimmed hard. Fruiting is limited further north, can be prolific in south.

Biodiversity An important source of pollen and nectar for insects in early spring. Fruit loved by birds and mammals, notably by Badgers, where piles of seeds can be found in their smelly latrines in autumn.

Threats No special threats.

A flowering hedge in early spring.

Fruits.

Flowers.

Wild Plum *Prunus domestica*

The Wild Plum is a natural hybrid between Cherry Plum and Blackthorn and has since been widely cultivated. Its genes have influenced the development of Domestic Plum, Bullace and Greengage.

Biology The earliest records of the species date from the first century, meaning Wild Plum is an archaeophyte, probably originally introduced for its fruit before becoming naturalised and widespread in the countryside.

Identification Common everywhere except Scottish Highlands and extreme west of Ireland, often in hedges. Grows up to 10m tall, bark purple-brown, roughly fissured. Buds long and pointed on hairless shoots. Leaves 8cm in length, wider beyond halfway, crinkled, downy on underside along veins. Flowers creamy white in mid-spring. Fruit small (4cm) plums, variously purple or yellow, edible, sweet and delicious. *Compare with Cherry Plum (p.185): buds shorter, fruit red or yellow.*

Culture Grows happily without any intervention, but rarely planted in this form (i.e. as opposed to garden plum cultivars). Can be cut hard and will regrow. Often suckers prolifically, creating dense thickets.

Biodiversity Flowers attract pollinating insects in spring. Fruits loved by resident and visiting thrushes. Small mammals gorge themselves before a hard winter.

Threats Aphids are particularly attracted to this species, as are sap-sucking brown scale insects and the larvae of the Plum Fruit Moth caterpillar. Silver leaf fungal disease can cause whole branches to die.

Crinkled leaves.

Maturing fruits.

Flowers.

Blackthorn *Prunus spinosa*

Our most fearsome thorny tree is a parent of Wild Plum, producing tart purple fruits known as sloes, popular when steeped in gin.

Biology Monoecious, producing single hermaphrodite flowers which are insect-pollinated. Fruits contain a single seed, distributed by birds and mammals. Also colonises by suckering.

Identification A viciously spined small tree to 7m, often suckering densely, creating impenetrable thickets. Bark dark purple-black, finely rough. Shoots initially downy becoming smooth, tips spined. Leaves wrinkled, initially downy becoming smooth, quite small (5cm), serrate margins. Flowers creamy white appearing before leaves. Fruits 15mm, purple becoming black.

Culture Blackthorn thrives almost everywhere but is especially tolerant of heavy clay soils. Can be included in a hedge which would deter any animal, but has tendency to spread outwards into arable fields and grassland. Can be laid, but beware its vicious thorns defeat even the thickest gloves and have a curious effect when penetrating the skin, causing instant pain and synovitis in and around joints (which disappears equally quickly when removed). Sloe berries are traditionally left until the first frost to be picked for culinary uses.

Biodiversity Flowers attract pollinators, fruits eaten by birds. Blackthorn is the larval food plant for at least 150 insect species, including Black Hairstreak and Brown Hairstreak butterflies and Swallow-tailed Moth.

Threats Generally a very robust species.

Fruits (sloes) persist into winter.

Blossom.

Maturing fruits.

Common Gorse *Ulex europaeus*

Common Gorse (or Furze) lights up the lower slopes of our uplands, heaths, abandoned pastures, sea cliffs and woodland rides with its bright golden-yellow flowers.

Biology A member of Fabaceae or the bean family. Monoecious, producing solitary pea-form flowers from January to June, which are insect-pollinated. Fruit is a bean-like pod containing 2–3 seeds which are forcibly ejected after the pod has hardened in the sun and split open suddenly on a hot day.

Identification Growing to 4m, evergreen shoots and leaves modified to form sharp green spines (seedlings have trifoliate leaves). Pea-like yellow flowers smell of coconut. *There are two other closely-related gorse species, both of which flower July to November. Western Gorse (Ulex gallii) is found in south-west England, Wales, and southern Éire on acid soils, growing up to 2m tall, wings of flower longer than its keel. Dwarf Gorse (Ulex minor) is mostly restricted to sandy heaths of southern England, up to 1m tall, flower wings and keel the same length.*

Culture Once widely planted for hedging, fodder and fuel.

Biodiversity Naturally a pioneer species, helping convert 'bare' ground to woodland, forming impenetrable thickets sheltering seedlings of other tree species. Its seeds are unharmed by fire, and plants can regenerate after wildfires. Thickets provide protection and nesting sites for birds, including Stonechat and Dartford Warbler.

Threats None.

Pea-like yellow flowers.

Spiny evergreen shoots.

Gorse scrub in spring.

Black Locust *Robinia pseudoacacia*

A contradictory species, it has several common names (including False Acacia and Robinia), possesses fragrant flowers alongside vicious thorns, and is able to restore damaged soils yet is sometimes considered invasive.

Biology A member of Fabaceae or the bean family, native to the south-eastern US where it grows alongside Black Walnut (p.119) and Tulip-tree (p.155), introduced sometime before 1640. Monoecious, producing pea-form flowers which are insect-pollinated. Seeds produced in bean-like pods (10cm), but main form of reproduction is vegetatively via root suckering.

Identification Medium-sized (up to 30m), often multi-stemmed with steeply ascending branches. Bark dark brown, becoming vertically fissured. Shoots with pairs of sharp thorns either side of buds. Leaves compound and pinnate, 9–23 leaflets with smooth margins, double thorns at leaf base (fold in wet weather and at night). Flowers white, hanging in cascades, with a sweet fragrance.

Culture A short-lived tree (60–100 years), and intolerant of shade so grows best on woodland edges and in clearings. Sensitive to late spring frosts, and not drought-tolerant. Nodules on its roots fix atmospheric nitrogen, fertilising neighbouring plants, making the tree useful in regenerating degraded soils. Can be coppiced. Timber hard and very durable for outdoor furniture, playgrounds and fenceposts. Caution should be applied when adding to a woodland, but makes a fine street tree.

Biodiversity No special associated biodiversity. Considered invasive in warmer European countries.

Threats Could thrive in a warming climate.

Shoots with opposite thorns, in pairs.

Bark vertically fissured.

Compound leaves, white flowers and seed pods.

Box *Buxus sempervirens*

Our slowest-growing tree, more usually seen as tightly clipped hedges and topiary in gardens, but in a few places grows wild in extraordinary dark and atmospheric thickets.

Biology Usually considered native to Britain (but contentious), restricted in natural stands to just a few locations in southern England, but widely cultivated in gardens across Britain and Ireland. Monoecious, producing inconspicuous yellow flowers without petals in early spring, insect-pollinated. Fruit a three-sided capsule containing 3–6 seeds, dispersed by ants (myrmecochory), which are attracted to nutrients attached to the seed (elaiosome).

Identification Grows to 10m tall, with a stem rarely larger than 15cm, dense and dark in form with winding stems. Bark pale brown, finely cracked and corky. Evergreen leaves small (3cm), dark green glossy, often with a notched tip, arranged opposite on shoots. Foliage is pungent, likened to cat urine, especially on warm days.

Culture Place names including 'box' suggest this species was once more widespread. Grows in understorey below other tree species, especially with European Beech and Yew, forming thickets. Stems grow slowly (1mm per two to three years), creating a very dense wood (the only homegrown timber that sinks in water). Fine-grained timber used for engraving, tool handles and wooden musical instruments.

Biodiversity Provides winter shelter to wildlife. A unique relationship with ants, especially red ants (*Myrmica* spp.).

Threats Two very serious threats can kill trees: Box-tree Moth (introduced pest arriving 2008), and a fungus known as box blight.

Side growth from an old stem.

Foliage and immature flowers.

Holly *Ilex aquifolium*

Once thought to provide protection from evil spirits, Holly has deep cultural connections for people while bringing welcome diversity to woodlands, especially in winter.

Biology Dioecious (separate male and female trees), both sexes bearing white flowers (males with four pistils, females with single style), insect-pollinated. Fruit is a drupe containing four seeds, eaten by birds and mammals and distributed in their droppings. Drooping lower branches can reproduce via layering.

Identification Very widespread, except central Scottish Highlands. Grows to 15m (rarely 20m) with pyramidal crown. Bark pale grey, often swirled with 'warts'. Leaves thick, glossy above, matt underside, margins highly variable: young trees and lower branches of older trees (to 2m) sharply spined, alternately upward/downward-facing points; upper leaves with smooth margins. Scarlet berries on female trees. There are many Holly cultivars, including some with variegated leaves.

Culture Dislikes very cold sites and waterlogged soils. Very shade-tolerant, although shade limits flowering. Highly palatable to deer, limiting growth and regeneration. Can be coppiced/pollarded, laid in hedges and layered. Pale and strong timber is highly sought after. Select female individuals for berries, which are mildly poisonous to humans.

Biodiversity A food plant for caterpillars of the Holly Blue butterfly. Berries require repeated frosts to soften and sweeten the fruit before becoming attractive to birds and mammals.

Threats Drought-resistant but fire-prone. Deer are the most significant threat.

Smooth, grey bark.

Glossy leaves, sharply spined, and white flowers.

Berries.

Field Maple *Acer campestre*

Once used by the Romans to support grape vines, this is the only maple native to Britain and is an ancient introduction to Ireland.

Biology Monoecious, producing hermaphrodite flowers (functioning as either male or female) in a corymb, mostly but not exclusively insect-pollinated. Fruits are double samaras, dispersed by gravity and wind.

Identification A medium tree (usually to 25m), less frequent in Ireland (where it is a neophyte) and the north of Scotland. Canopy densely branched and twiggy. Bark pale brown, becoming corky with small square plates. Shoots can develop corky ridges (like Field Elm p.151), with opposite arranged brown-coloured buds. Leaves dark green, with veins radiating from base to 3–5 slightly rounded lobes, margins with a few large teeth, turning yellow in autumn. Flowers yellow-green, without petals. Double-winged seeds have crimson-coloured wings arranged almost at 180 degrees. *Compare with Sycamore (p.203): buds green, leaves more pointed and toothed. Compare with Norway Maple (p.201): leaf margins more toothed, whiskers at tips.*

Culture Thrives on heavy and fertile soils, especially in lowlands. Extremely shade-tolerant when young, but later needs more light. Commonly grows mixed with other broadleaves. Autumn foliage is particularly attractive along woodland edges and as standard trees in hedgerows.

Biodiversity Many insects benefit from feeding on its pollen, while foliage is attractive to larvae of many moths. Small mammals feast on fallen seeds.

Threats Generally robust and healthy.

Double-winged samaras.

Buds grow in opposite pairs.

Leaves with rounded lobes.

Norway Maple *Acer platanoides*

Tolerant of pollution with rich autumn colours, Norway Maple is a good choice for 'greening' our towns and cities, and may yet prove popular in future forests.

Biology Native to much of Europe including many neighbouring countries, this species was introduced surprisingly late, in 1683. Monoecious, hermaphrodite flowers, mainly insect-pollinated. Fruits are double samaras, dispersed by gravity and wind.

Identification Often with a broad-domed canopy, up to 30m. Bark grey and quite smooth until older. Shoots smooth with opposite red-brown buds, when broken exude a milky latex (unlike other featured maples). Leaves green, with veins radiating from base to five lobes, margins with large teeth and whiskered tips, turning yellow in autumn (rarely red). Flowers yellow-green in upright corymbs. Double-winged seeds at 90 degrees. There are several cultivars selected for various leaf colourations.

Culture A cold-hardy species but does not tolerate exposure, unlike Sycamore (p.203). Its endurance to pollution and colourful autumn foliage means it is a good choice for urban planting schemes. In a forest it can regenerate very effectively (even becoming invasive) where herbivores are controlled. Its timber is not widely available but could be more popular as a productive forest species, being a pale, smooth, close-grained hardwood.

Biodiversity Sometimes considered invasive. Flowers attract pollinating insects.

Threats Vulnerable to bark stripping by Grey Squirrels. Also affected by various leaf spot and blotch diseases.

Autumn leaf colour.

Bark grey and smooth.

Leaves have five sharp-pointed lobes.

Sycamore *Acer pseudoplatanus*

This is the largest maple in Britain (known as Plane in Scotland) and one of our hardiest trees, such as the individual growing on Hadrian's Wall on the England–Scotland border which became world famous when it was illegally felled.

Biology Neophyte and widely naturalised. Monoecious, yellow-green flowers hanging from pendulous panicles, insect-pollinated. Fruits are double samaras, dispersed by gravity and wind.

Identification Large (to 40m) tall with spreading canopy of sweeping branches, found on exposed coasts, mixed broadleaved woods, and as scattered trees in upland farmland. Bark grey with plates. Shoots brown-grey and stout, buds opposite and green, turning red as they flush. Leaves large (20cm), single, palmate, five-pointed margins with many coarse teeth. Flower panicles to 12cm, producing double-winged seeds at 90 degrees.

Culture This species requires little or no encouragement to thrive in almost any situation and under any management regime. Produces an excellent pale and attractive hardwood timber. Valuable trees have beautiful ripple figure (e.g. 'fiddleback' used in making musical string instruments).

Biodiversity Sycamore polarises opinion among conservationists, being appreciated for its support of hundreds of insect species while providing a niche for wildlife associated with the threatened Common Ash, yet disliked for its tendency to repress ground flora. Sticky drips from leaves are caused by 'honeydew' produced by feeding aphids.

Threats Vulnerable to bark stripping by Grey Squirrels. Leaves often visibly infected by tar-spot fungus but not harmful. However, sooty bark disease can kill trees.

Bark grey with plates.

Buds opposite, turning red when flushing.

Flower panicle and developing winged seeds.

Horse Chestnut *Aesculus hippocastanum*

Introduced in the early 1600s from the Balkans and often known simply as a 'Conker Tree', Horse Chestnut is among our most flamboyant trees, with showy white flower clusters.

Biology Monoecious, 20–50 flowers produced on each upright panicle, hermaphrodite flowers at base, becoming male towards tip. Insect-pollinated, especially bees. Only 2–5 flowers at base produce fruit, a spiky husk protecting 2–3 nuts ('conkers') inside until mature. Seeds dispersed by gravity and mammals.

Identification Tall (35m) and broad-domed (20m wide) canopy, with heavy, sweeping branches. Grows in recreation grounds, parks and large gardens, but occasionally woodland edges. Bark grey, becoming rough and scaly with age. Shoots with horseshoe-shaped leaf scars, buds red-brown, sticky. Leaves palmate, compound, leaflets (5–7) radiating from a central point with no stalks. Flowers in distinctive upright clumps, petals white with basal spots at first yellow, then blushed pink. *Compare with Indian Horse Chestnut (not featured): leaflets with stalks, flowers pink, fruit husks smooth.*

Culture Prefers deep, well-drained soils, tolerates pollution and exposed sites, although its heavy branches are easily damaged by summer winds (when the dense foliage acts like a sail). Its timber is inferior, even as a fuelwood. Conkers remain popular in the traditional combative game. Seeds are poisonous to humans and horses.

Biodiversity A good source of nectar for insects. Holes created by broken limbs provide nesting sites for birds like the Jackdaw.

Threats The Horse Chestnut Leaf Miner can affect tree growth and regeneration.

Palmate, compound leaf with 5–7 leaflets.

Spiny cupules containing conkers.

Underside showing leaf miner damage.

Purging Buckthorn *Rhamnus cathartica*

This may be one of our most easily overlooked small trees, found growing in hedgerows among other species, but it attracts one of our brightest butterflies, the bright yellow Brimstone.

Biology Dioecious, inconspicuous yellow-green flowers of both sexes, insect-pollinated. Fruit a berry (drupe), containing 2–4 seeds. Distributed by birds and small mammals.

Identification Most common in central and southern England, but easily overlooked. Grows on alkaline (calcareous) soils, to 10m tall. Stem often very short (less than 1m), branches above being untidy and twiggy in appearance. Bark dark brown, small scales. Shoots slender grey-brown, side shoots often ending in a sharp spine. Buds dark-brown, appressed, usually opposite, but sometimes staggered even alternate. Leaves small (6cm), dark green, veins curving forwards, small rounded teeth on margins towards tip. Yellow-green flowers appear at base of shoots. Small (10mm)

black globular fruits. *Compare with Dogwood (p.217).*

Culture Very shade-tolerant, and a hardy tree. Tendency to sucker can be a problem when growing in hedgerows, spreading into neighbouring fields. Roots produce a compound (emodin) with allelopathic effects, reducing competition from other plants. Both bark and fruits can irritate human skin, although once an important herbal medicine, including as a strong purgative (hence the tree's common name). Just a few berries can have a significant laxative effect (children should avoid).

Biodiversity A main larval food plant for the Brimstone butterfly. Fruit remains on tree long into the winter, sustaining many birds.

Threats None.

Often multi-stemmed.

Black, globular fruits.

Leaf veins curve forwards towards tip.

Alder Buckthorn *Frangula alnus*

Charcoal made using the yellow timber of this small tree was once a prime choice for gunpowder manufacture, and 'Swiss black powder' is still used today in fireworks and historical firearm reenactments.

Biology Monoecious, hermaphrodite flowers insect-pollinated. Fruit a berry (drupe), containing 2–3 seeds. Distributed by birds and small mammals.

Identification Uncommon across much of Scotland, but otherwise found on acid soils, often on heathlands and fringes of wetland. Typically a very short stem (1m), slender branching above, reaching 6m tall. Bark smooth grey. Shoots straight, reddish-brown with white streaks made by elongated lenticels. Buds scale-less, alternate. Leaves small (5cm) with smooth margins, blunt tips. Flowers tiny (5mm) with five green petals, star-like. Fruit 10mm, red ripening to dark purple, persisting on the tree into the winter.

Culture A hardy tree which will grow under varied conditions, very shade-tolerant. Tendency to sucker can be a problem when growing in hedges. Its timber is brittle, but shoots were once popular for butchers' skewers, given their straightness. Most parts of the tree are considered poisonous, yet it has long been used as a traditional medicine, whose laxative effects are more gentle than those of Purging Buckthorn.

Biodiversity A main larval food plant for the Brimstone butterfly. Fruit remains on tree long into the winter, sustaining many birds, especially Fieldfare, Redwing and Waxwing.

Threats None.

Short stem with grey bark.

Star-like five-petalled flowers.

Leaves have smooth margins, blunt tips.

Small-leaved Lime   *Tilia cordata*

One of our 'youngest' native trees, arriving long after the ice sheet retreated, Small-leaved Lime soon became an important species culturally, and a good indicator of ancient woodland.

Biology Native to England and Wales, probably an archaeophyte in Scotland and Ireland. Monoecious, with clusters of 5–8 hermaphrodite flowers, insect-pollinated. Fruit a drupe, with the appearance of a dry nut containing 1–2 seeds, attached to a persistent papery bract which acts as a wing, wind-dispersed, capable of moving 300m. Also reproduces by suckering and layering.

Identification Tall domed tree (40m), but can be narrow in competition with other trees, also coppice or pollard. Bark grey-brown with long vertical fissures. Shoots hairless, brown or sometimes red, hairless buds with distinctive large central and smaller side scale. Leaves (8cm), hairless except red tufts under vein axils, underside paler than upperside, margin serrated. Flowers in stiff upright sprays, yellow-green (June–July) and plentiful, changing the appearance of the whole tree and smelling sweetly. Fruits in clusters of 5–8 attached to a bract, globules with a thin, smooth coat, easily cracked open. *Compare with Large-leaved Lime (p.213). Compare with European Lime (*Tilia × europaea, *not featured): tufts under leaves pale brown, flowers droop.*

Culture Thrives in well-drained loamy soils. Traditionally managed as coppice in forests, where old stools are an indicator of ancient woodland. Pale timber is stable and easily shaped. Inner bark is highly fibrous, once harvested as 'bast' for rope-making.

Biodiversity Its flowers attract a myriad of insects, especially bees and hoverflies.

Threats Generally healthy. Attracts browsers, especially deer. A warming climate might help extend its range northwards.

Yellow-green flowers with green bract.

Leaf, margin serrated.

Ancient coppice.

Large-leaved Lime *Tilia platyphyllos*

An elegant tree for parks and stately avenues, yet not always popular as a street tree due to the sticky deposits of honeydew from feeding aphids.

Biology Native to Britain (specifically England and Wales), a neophyte in Ireland, but quite uncommon where not planted, naturally occurring on calcareous rocky outcrops, screes and on cliffs. Monoecious, with clusters of 3–6 hermaphrodite flowers, insect-pollinated. Fruit a drupe, with the appearance of a dry nut containing 1–2 seeds, attached to a persistent papery bract which acts as a wing, wind-dispersed. Also reproduces by suckering and layering.

Identification Tall domed tree (40m), also coppice or pollard. Bark grey-brown and smooth. Shoots grey, sometimes red, buds with three scales, partially haired. Leaves (12 cm), covered in soft hairs, including petioles, margin serrated and sides can flop. Flowers hang, yellow-green (June–July), smelling sweetly. Fruits in clusters 3–6 from a bract, globules with a thick, ridged coat, difficult to crack open. Frequently hybridises with Small-leaved Lime, producing the fertile European or Common Lime. *Compare with Small-leaved Lime (p.211): bark smoother, leaves larger and hairy, flowers erect.*

Culture A very robust and long-lived species, capable of competing with other large broadleaves thanks to its deep roots. An important species for honey production in some parts of Europe.

Biodiversity Flowers are pollinated by bees, hoverflies and butterflies, notably the Lime Hawk-moth. Infections with Lime Nail Gall Mites (appearance of red nails hammered through the leaf) are unmissable.

Threats Generally healthy, including resistance to honey fungus. Attracts browsers, especially deer.

Lime nail galls.

Bark grey-brown, quite smooth.

Flowers yellow-green, hanging in clusters.

Sea Buckthorn *Hippophae rhamnoides*

An important species, helping to stabilise coastal sand dunes, while nitrogen-fixing nodules on its roots help improve fertility, encouraging other tree species such as Common Hawthorn (p.163) and Elder (p.225) to colonise.

Biology Native in Britain, probably only the east coast of England, and elsewhere a widely planted neophyte. The only tree species within a recognised dune-scrub habitat, typically growing with marram grass. Dioecious, wind-pollinated. Fruit a drupe, distributed by feeding birds.

Identification Thorny small tree, rarely more than 6m tall, on sand dunes but widely planted elsewhere, including as a garden plant. Bark and branches dark brown and rough-textured, spines frequent. Shoots covered with silver scales, buds orange. Leaves lance-shaped, dull green upperside, silvery scaled underside. Flowers tiny and yellow-green (September–February), female plants producing clusters of orange berry-like fruits.

Culture Widely cultivated and planted, sometimes considered invasive outside of its natural habitat (e.g. mobile dunes). Used to improve soil fertility in land reclamation or agroforestry. Berries are rich with vitamins and natural oils, which are sometimes harvested for use in jellies and syrups.

Biodiversity Forms important coastal scrub habitat for migrant and breeding birds, including Fieldfare and Redwing, which feast on its fruit.

Threats Generally healthy.

Berry-like orange drupes.

Leaves lance-shaped, silvery.

Dogwood *Cornus sanguinea*

A small tree with brightly coloured stems, producing fragrant flowers in spring and small black berries much loved by birds in winter.

Biology Monoecious with numerous hermaphrodite flowers in a flat-topped inflorescence, growing from the tip of shoots. Insect-pollinated, forming panicles with multiple drupes (fruit) each with a single seed. Distributed by birds and small mammals. Readily suckers, propagating clonally.

Identification A bushy small tree (rarely to 10m tall), with straight branches but repeatedly forking. Bark grey and smooth. Shoots thin, green to red (especially in sunlight). Buds scale-less, opposite. Leaves in opposite pairs, green sometimes blushed red, veins curving forward, turning red-purple in autumn. Flowers borne on shoot tips means new shoots must grow from a pair of buds behind, causing repeated forking. Flowers fragrant, yellowish or creamy white, in flat-topped clusters. Fruit in clusters of purple-black (7mm) 'berries'. *Compare with Purging Buckthorn (p.207): leaf vein pattern similar but margins toothed.* Many cultivars available, such as the colourful 'Midwinter Fire'.

Culture Thrives in many soil types and conditions. Partially shade-tolerant, often found along edges of woodlands and hedgerows. Tendency to sucker can be problematic when planted next to fields and meadows as it quickly spreads. Its straight sticks were used as butchers' skewers and in arrow-making. Thin and colourful stems popular for weaving.

Biodiversity Fragrant flowers attract bees, hoverflies and other pollinating insects. Berries popular among small birds.

Threats Generally healthy, notably resistant to honey fungus.

Clusters of white flowers.

Fruits small, black.

Autumn colours.

Strawberry-tree *Arbutus unedo*

An attractive small tree, known as Caithne in Éire, where it holds special cultural significance. Produces red strawberry-like fruits.

Biology A Mediterranean species, currently listed as native in Ireland but disputed. Its distribution follows patterns of ancient copper mining, so possibly imported by Bronze Age miners travelling from northern Spain 4,000 years ago (i.e. an archaeophyte). Monoecious, female and male flowers produced in hanging inflorescences, insect-pollinated. Fruit a berry with 25 seeds, distributed by birds. A natural hybrid (*Arbutus* × *andrachnoides*) is an occasional street tree, growing to 10m, red-stemmed.

Identification A small (7m) tree, with dense, rounded clumps of bright green evergreen foliage. Often found growing on steep, rocky ground, including cliffs. Bark red-brown, peeling. Leaves glossy and leathery, rounded serrated margins.

Flowers ivory with pink blushing, bell-shaped, blooming through winter. Fruits take one year to mature, turning green-yellow to red, strawberry-like, hence its common name (but perhaps more like a lychee).

Culture A hardy pioneer species, capable of growing in many sites (sometimes considered invasive). Regenerates readily, even after severe cutting, sprouting from lignotubers. Fruit edible but not tasty to humans unless cooked, though loved by birds.

Biodiversity Flowers provide a valuable source of nectar through winter months.

Threats Generally free of serious pests and pathogens. Natural populations in Ireland may be at threat due to their isolation.

Red-brown bark.

Strawberry-like fruits.

Bright green, evergreen foliage.

Common Ash *Fraxinus excelsior*

One of our most common broadleaved trees, often considered the queen among our native trees. Now under widespread threat from a deadly fungal disease.

Biology The only ash species native to Britain and Ireland, with two close relatives native to the rest of Europe: Narrow-leaved Ash and Manna Ash. Common Ash trees are monoecious but often change gender over time. Wind-pollinated. Winged samara distributed by wind. Very effective at natural regeneration, with densely growing seedlings appearing below parent trees.

Identification Large (30m) broadleaved tree with sparse branches. Leaves compound, 9–13 leaflets all stalkless, except tip leaflet, serrated margins. Black buds in opposite pairs, mitre-shaped. Flowers purple-black clusters. Distinctive winged seed 'keys' (samaras). *Compare with Elder (p.225), Common Walnut (p.121) and Rowan (p.167).*

Culture Prefers fertile well-drained soils, thriving in valley sides. Grows in mixed woodlands with other broadleaves but does not tolerate shade. Sensitive to late spring frosts. When young, prune to single forks to improve tree form.

Biodiversity 955 taxa associated, including 45 obligate. Host to many lichens, which are adapted to its acidic bark. Older trees with deadwood are a favourite among woodpeckers, while canopies offer nest sites for Rooks.

Threats Main threat is dieback caused by the fungus *Hymenoscyphus fraxineus*. Look for lens-shaped lesion on young stems and branches, followed by wilting. Possible future threat from Emerald Ash Borer, now present in mainland Europe.

Compound, pinnate leaves with 9–13 leaflets.

The winged samaras hang in large clusters.

Flowers in early spring.

Indian Bean *Catalpa bignonioides*

Introduced in 1726 from the Deep South of the US, where it is known as Southern Catalpa, it has since become a popular street tree on account of its showy flowers and distinctive 'bean pods'.

Biology Confusingly does not originate from India (earning its name from the original name given to Indigenous peoples by European explorers), but does grow 'beans'! Monoecious, bearing hermaphrodite flowers in racemes, insect-pollinated. Flowers borne on untidy panicles. Fruit a long capsule, splitting open to release seeds with long hairs that aid wind dispersal.

Identification Growing up to 15m tall, and equally wide, often leaning with twisted branches. Bark noticeably colourful, from pink-brown to orange. Shoots grey-brown, buds orange and often in threes, shoot tip typically shrivelled in appearance because it does not produce a terminal bud and is often damaged by autumn frosts. Leaves very large (30cm), heart-shaped at base, hairy underside, abrupt pointed tips, smells pungent when crushed. Flowers white with purple and yellow centres, borne on 'candles', little fragrance. 'Bean pods' thin, up to 40cm. *Compare with Foxglove Tree (*Paulownia tomentosa, *not featured): leaves even larger, hairy on both surfaces and without abrupt pointed tip, flowers fragrant purple bells.*

Culture Very frost-sensitive, so avoid cold sites and hollows. Prefers full sun and well-drained soils. Can be pruned hard when dormant.

Biodiversity Flowers attract pollinating insects.

Threats Frost damage. Susceptible to verticillium wilt and moderately to honey fungus.

Colourful bark.

Large heart-shaped leaves and 'bean pods'.

Elder *Sambucus nigra*

The ultimate survivor, colonising abandoned industrial land, railway sidings and farmyards, Elder (sometimes 'Elderberry') dazzles in spring and provides a bountiful autumn harvest for wildlife.

Biology Monoecious, producing hermaphrodite flowers in wide corymbs. Insect-pollinated, producing clusters of fruits (berries). Distributed by birds and frugivorous mammals.

Identification Typically multi-stemmed, to 10m. Stems grow rapidly and tend to arch over. Bark pale fawn, corky. Shoots with raised 'warts' with prominent lenticels, hollow when young. Buds opposite pairs, purple, spiky scales. Leaves compound pinnate, 5–7 leaflets with serrated margin, smell when crushed. Flowers cream-white saucers of tiny flowers, fragrance sweet-scented. Black berries hang on red stalks, in clusters like miniature grapes.

Culture Elder needs little help from humans to thrive. It is even resistant to Rabbits (hence often found growing next to warrens) and even as an epiphyte, growing in the hollows of old trees of other species. Typically quite short-lived (30–60 years), but coppicing older trees can rejuvenate them. Flower sprays traditionally collected to make homemade 'champagne', or commercially to make a refreshing cordial. Berries are poisonous to humans without cooking.

Biodiversity Attracts invertebrates to its flowers, especially hoverflies and beetles. Birds love to feast on the berries. Jelly Ear fungus commonly found on stems.

Threats None.

Pale, corky bark.

Fruits (berries) on red stalks.

Saucers of tiny, cream-white flowers.

Elder – Angiosperms

Wayfaring-tree *Viburnum lantana*

A small tree which is abundant along the sides of tracks and paths, and therefore a constant companion to the wayfarer (someone travelling on foot).

Biology Native to southern England and parts of Wales, a neophyte elsewhere in Britain and Ireland. Monoecious, hermaphrodite flowers growing as a rounded cyme, insect-pollinated. Fruit an oblong drupe (8mm), containing a single seed, distributed by birds and small mammals.

Identification Small tree (to 6m), usually a dense mass of multiple stems. Prefers warm, sunny conditions, hence its restricted range in Britain and Ireland. Bark pale brown, developing rough plates. Shoots downy, buds opposite and naked. Leaves single, crinkled appearance, serrated margins, densely downy and pale undersides. Tiny white flowers with five petals and protruding yellow stigma, in dense round-headed clusters (10cm) of multiple flowers, all similarly sized, slightly pungent. Fruits in tight bunches, first green then scarlet, maturing to black.

Culture Initially shade-tolerant when young, but soon needs full sun. Tends to grow particularly well on alkaline soils (e.g. limestone and chalk). Impervious to Rabbits, so often found around warrens. Raw fruits are mildly poisonous to humans. Flexible stems were once put to good use in tying, skewering and weaving.

Biodiversity Flowers have little nectar (hence unpleasant smell), so attractive mainly to pollen-harvesting insects. Fruits attract thrushes and other small birds.

Threats Generally healthy, even resistant to browsing deer.

Pale brown bark with rough plates.

Fruits mature from scarlet to black.

Round-headed clusters of tiny white flowers.

Guelder-rose *Viburnum opulus*

Our most showy native tree, bearing elegant sharp-lobed leaves, which turn fiery red in autumn while bearing glossy jewel-like fruits through the winter.

Biology Native to Britain and Ireland, though less frequent in Scotland, thriving in damp woodland. Monoecious, with hermaphrodite flowers in a complex compound cyme, with an outer ring of large (20mm) sterile flowers whose only function is to attract insect pollinators to the small (6mm) quite inconspicuous inner ring of fertile flowers. Fruit is a fleshy drupe containing a single flattened seed, only maturing in midwinter and remaining attached. Distributed by birds during winter.

Identification A short bushy tree (4m) found on damp, heavy soils, usually with multiple low, sweeping branches which throw up multiple vertical shoots. Bark and branches grey-brown, angular. Shoots bear long ridges, green-yellow buds in opposite pairs, with a tiny terminal bud. Leaves have 3–5 sharp lobes with irregular shallow dentate margins, three veins at base. Distinctive white flowerheads (10cm) with outer ring of larger showy flowers. Glossy red fruits in clusters of 10 or more. *Compare leaves to Sycamore (p.203) and Field Maple (p.199): both have more than three veins at leaf base.*

Culture Tolerates heavy shade but requires some sunlight to flower. Fruit is mildly poisonous to humans unless cooked.

Biodiversity Fruit is highly desired by some birds, especially Song Thrush and Bullfinch, as a valuable food source in late winter.

Threats Foliage highly palatable to deer.

Glossy red fruits in clusters.

Grey-brown bark and sharp-lobed leaves.

Flowerheads have outer ring of large showy flowers.

Spindle *Euonymus europaeus*

Easily overlooked through most of the year, Spindle is unmissable in autumn with its rich leaf colours and uniquely gaudy fruits in a 'sunset-glow' combination of bright pink and orange.

Biology Gynodioecious (some trees female, others hermaphrodite), producing cymes of 3–10 flowers. Insect-pollinated, producing capsule fruits containing a fleshy pseudo-aril around a single seed. Distributed by birds and small mammals.

Identification A small tree (8m), usually with many 'leggy' branches. Bark grey and quite smooth with long vertical fissures. Shoots green and smooth initially, later developing four brown ridges of rougher texture (giving the stem a square-like appearance). Buds opposite. Leaves elliptical, margins finely serrated. Flowers (April–July) cream-green in loose clusters. Fruits (10mm) with four angled lobes, green turning bright pink, opening to reveal a fleshy orange layer (pseudo-aril) containing a single white seed.

Culture Prefers well-drained and alkaline soils, and while partially shade-tolerant, Spindle thrives best in full sun. It makes a colourful addition to woodland edges and hedgerows. Its timber, rarely available in large diameters, was once used for making spindles, combs and toothpicks. It makes a very good drawing charcoal. Many parts of the tree are poisonous, including the bark and seed.

Biodiversity Fruits attract a range of small birds and mammals. Larvae of the Spindle Ermine moth feed on foliage in early summer, producing distinctive 'webs' in the branches.

Threats None. Spindle Ermine can completely defoliate trees, but trees generally recover.

Grey bark with notable long fissures.

Leaves and immature fruits.

Mature fruits, pink with orange insides.

Glossary

Technical terms used to describe botanical features to help with identification are described separately, see Botanical terms (p.15).

Term	Description
allelopathic	the chemical inhibition of one plant by another due to the release of compounds which inhibit germination or growth (e.g. juglone in Walnut, emodin in Purging Buckthorn).
arboriculture	cultivation, management and study of individual trees, practised by an arboriculturist, arborist or tree surgeon. (*see also* forestry).
archaeophyte	a non-native tree species considered an 'ancient introduction', technically from prehistory up to 1500 (*see also* neophyte).
associated biodiversity	the variety of wildlife, beyond the individual host, that is found within and around a tree(s) of that species, sometimes very closely dependent on that species.
brashed/brashing	the removal of lower (up to 2m) branches of trees, especially in conifer plantations, to improve access.
canker	an area of dead tissue on a tree, often appearing as sunken, discoloured or cracked; often arising from damage caused by fungal or bacterial pathogens.
canopy	the foliar cover from the crowns of trees in a forest stand, which can consist of several layers.
clone/clonal	a plant produced from asexual propagation, making it identical to the original material. Production of such material is termed clonal propagation, which can be natural (e.g. suckering) or artificial (i.e. undertaken by people).
coppice	(v.) to cut the stem of a tree near its base to stimulate the production of multiple new stems; (n.) a coppice stool. Also (n.) an area of coppice (*see also* pollard).
crown	part of a tree consisting of branches, leaves and flowers.
epiphyte	a tree which grows on the surface of another tree, deriving water and nutrients from its surface or hollows.
flush/flushing	when leaf buds open in spring.
forestry	the art, science and practice of creating, managing and conserving natural and humanmade forests (*see also* arboriculture).
graft	a form of clonal propagation where a cutting from one part of a tree (called a scion) is inserted into another part of a tree with roots (the rootstock).
habitat	the natural environment where animals and plants live together.
horticulture	the art or practice of garden and orchard cultivation and management (*see also* forestry; arboriculture).

layering	a form of vegetative propagation, either natural or initiated by people, in which a branch contacts the soil and develops roots.
leader	a main, dominant vertical stem, usually at the top of the tree.
mast	a collective for seeds. Also: a year in which there is abundant production of seed.
native	a tree species which arrived naturally in Britain and Ireland after the end of the last glaciation (i.e. without the assistance of humans) or one that was already present (i.e. it persisted during the last Ice Age) (*see also* non-native).
neophyte	a non-native tree species considered a 'recent introduction', technically introduced to Britain and Ireland after the discovery of the New World in about 1550 (*see also* archaeophyte).
non-native	a tree species that was introduced either deliberately or accidentally by humans, sometimes called 'alien' or exotic. Further divided into archaeophyte and neophyte.
pioneer	a tree species which first colonises a new habitat following a disturbance, such as grazing or fire.
pollard	(v.) to cut the stem of a tree at about human head height to stimulate the production of multiple new stems out of the reach of browsing domestic livestock or deer, to create (n.) a pollard (*see also* coppice).
provenance	the geographic origin of a source of tree material, including seed, seedlings or pollen.
pruning	the removal of shoots and branches from a tree, either naturally (self-pruning caused by shading) or through active management, both formative pruning (correction of trees less than 2m tall by the removal of competing shoots or singling of forked stems) and high pruning (removal of branches above 2m to improve timber quality).
refugia	areas in which a population of trees survive through a period of unfavourable conditions, especially glaciation and expansion of ice sheets.
standard	a large tree, in forestry usually meaning a specimen managed for timber often growing above coppice, or in arboriculture meaning a tree that has been trained to develop a single, straight and clean trunk, typically around 1.8m, before branches develop.
stool	the stump of a tree when coppiced.
sucker(ing)	a shoot that arises at or below ground level from a tree stem or root, common in some species and which may be encouraged by certain management activities. It is a form of clonal propagation.
timber	wood that has been processed from a tree for a variety of purposes (e.g. construction, furniture etc.).
veneer	a thinly sliced timber product, typically cut by slicing or rotary peeling high-value and attractive timbers for use in prestige products (e.g. furniture-making, car dashboards).
windfirm	a tree with the ability to withstand strong winds.

Further reading

Hemery, G. (2023). *The Forest Guide Scotland: Copses, Woods and Forests*. Bloomsbury Wildlife.

Hemery, G. (2025). *The Forest Guide Wales: Copses, Woods and Forests*. Bloomsbury Wildlife.

Hemery, G. (2026). *The Forest Guide England: Copses, Woods and Forests*. Bloomsbury Wildlife.

Hemery, G. and Simblet, S. (2021). *The New Sylva: A Discourse of Forest and Orchard Trees for the Twenty-First Century*. 2nd ed. Bloomsbury Publishing.

Stroh, P.A., Humphrey, T.A., Burkmar, R.J., Pescott, O.L., Roy, D.B. and Walker, K.J. (2020). *BSBI Online Plant Atlas 2020*. Botanical Society of Britain and Ireland. plantatlas2020.org/atlas

Resources

Tree health

- **Observatree:** an early warning system for tree health in the UK where volunteers can help spot new threats. observatree.org.uk
- Online reporting tools for tree pests and diseases allowing anyone to report a concern:
  - **TreeAlert** (Britain). treealert.forestresearch.gov.uk
  - **TreeCheck** (Ireland). treecheck.net

Wildlife recording

There are many websites and apps now available to help nature lovers learn more about the natural world, and also contribute to science.

- **iRecord:** a website and app allowing anyone to record a wildlife sighting in Britain and Ireland. Photo recognition software helps with an initial ID, which is then checked by experts, while data supports research and monitoring, including national recording schemes. irecord.org.uk
- **iNaturalist:** similar to iRecord but with a global geographical scope, and relies on its community of enthusiasts to support verification. inaturalist.org

Other

- **Plant Atlas 2020:** an online version of the Plant Atlas of the BSBI, providing helpful information about plants found in Britain and Ireland. plantatlas2020.org

A leaf-rolling weevil at work on Aspen.

Acknowledgements

I am indebted to Andrew Smith and Forestry Commission staff at Westonbirt Arboretum and Bedgebury Pinetum for their support during research, and for permissions to capture some of the images used in this guide.

Compiling a guide like this would be impossible without the enthusiasm and expertise of amateur naturalists across Britain and Ireland. Therefore the volunteers and county recorders of the Botanical Society of Britain and Ireland deserve a special mention. I thank John McLoughlin for a good debate about the native status of the Strawberry-tree in Ireland.

I would also like to thank my commissioning editor, Julie Bailey, and project editors Amy Hodkin and Kate Dickinson, at Bloomsbury; designer Austin Taylor; copyeditor Lucy Beevor; proofreader Marianne Taylor; and the team at the RSPB.

Finally, I am grateful to my wife Jane for her loving support while I conducted the fieldwork and writing of this guide.

Photo credits

All the photographs in this book were taken by the author, Gabriel Hemery, with the exception of the following. Bloomsbury Publishing would like to thank the following for providing photographs and for permission to reproduce copyright material within this book.

KEY: t=top, l=left, r=right, bl=bottom left, br=bottom right, SS=Shutterstock, Alamy=Alamy Stock Photo.

33 t Roger Thornby/iStock; **43** br Katerina Dalemans/SS; **52** Matt_Gibson/iStock; **58** Stocktopia Life/Alamy; 75 r Victoria Sharratt/SS; **85** r Greens and Blues/SS; **86** gbs097/iStock; **89** l Peter Turner Photography/SS; **90** Janet dharma/SS; **96** Wirestock Creators/SS; **97** l grisdee/SS, r Brzostowska/SS; **112** Müller/McPhoto/Alamy; **141** l Photo Central/Alamy; **147** bl Hartmut Goldhahn/SS; **160** Jim Laws/Alamy; **168** Manfred Ruckszio/SS; **169** l nortivision/SS, tr ChWeiss/SS, br Wirestock Creators/SS; **186** Ed Buziak/Alamy; **208** piemags/nature/Alamy; **215** l Blooms Heart/SS; **223** r Peter Turner Photography/SS; **226** Rob Read/Alamy; **228** Brian Hoffman/Alamy.

About the author

Gabriel Hemery is a writer, photographer and forest scientist. He co-founded and is chief executive of Sylva Foundation, a charity caring for forests across Britain. He is author of *The New Sylva*, published by Bloomsbury in 2014 (republished in 2021). He has also written a series of three guidebooks, *The Forest Guides*, published by Bloomsbury Wildlife and featuring the copses, woods and forests of Scotland (2023), Wales (2025) and England (2026). gabrielhemery.com

Index

Tree species: common names

Tree species: scientific names